you only *think* **God** is silent

HEARING GOD

in the **defining moments** *of Our Lives*

JULIE ANN ALLEN

To: Carrie & Patti
His Peace be with you

TATE PUBLISHING, LLC

This book is designed to provide accurate and authoritative information
with regard to the subject matter covered. This information is given with the
understanding that neither the author nor Tate Publishing, LLC is engaged
in rendering legal, professional advice. Since the details of your situation
are fact dependent, you should additionally seek the services of a competent
professional.

ISBN: 1-5988600-0-3

This book is dedicated
to
the glory of God

Acknowledgements

There are not enough pages in any book to hold the expressions of gratitude I feel for all of those who have been the hands and feet of God for me and my children in these times. The list of those I would like to acknowledge is not complete in these words, but some must be mentioned.

I want to thank my children who have been my reason to get up on the hardest mornings, my source of laughter on the days I did not want to laugh, and who are the best part of my every day. You always understood when I needed to sit at the computer and when I told you that God wanted me to do this . . . and you never complained.

I want to thank my parents, my sister and her husband, and my brother and his wife. Your love, support, understanding, tears, hugs, and listening ears are more than any one could ever hope for and are generously given to us constantly. You bless us more than words can say.

I want to thank my Uncle Rich and Aunt Jane who stayed with me at my house to prevent a first night alone before I was ready . . . and for so much love and support.

To my late husband's parents and sisters, I thank God for you and the family you are to us now and in the years to come.

Thank you to Patti Gaffney and her family. For the years you have invested in us, for the love you have given us, for all that you are to us, I thank God!

Thank you to Mika Simpson and Beth Ussery for moving into my home during the week of chaos and into my life in the days and years afterward. You bless me with your friendship!

A huge thank you to my constant army of support that is the action team for God: David, Cindy, Andrew and Mandy Hall, Keith Shumaker, Mark Shumaker, Paul and Sarah Hudson,

Charlie and Deb Foreman, Ed and Laurie Bolden, and a very long list of amazing servants of God who have done countless, selfless acts to keep our family's home together.

I want to thank the entire church family at Heritage United Methodist Church for loving us before this happened, sustaining us as this happened, and nurturing and understanding us as we moved forward. I will always treasure the years of ministry I spent with you and miss you as God moves us forward.

I want to thank the church family at White's Chapel United Methodist Church for taking us in and loving us when healing meant it was time to find a new worship home.

I owe a debt of gratitude to Ron Reed, Whitney Smith, Cynthia Eaton, and Britt Monts for your generous gifts of support, self, expertise, guidance, and assurances that gave me the ability to see the bright future God promised.

I am so grateful for the faculty and staff where I teach and to the other choir directors in the district for their many acts of kindness and support. I am thankful for my students who never gave up on me . . . even when my bad days outnumbered my good days. A thank you to Marie and Pam for encouraging me to write and affirming me along the way, and Cheryl, you will never know how much I treasure our friendship!

I want to thank my neighbors and the community and the many–beyond number–who helped, donated, prayed, watched, and acted on God's behalf to make certain I always knew that I was not alone.

Finally, I want to thank those of you who have asked "Where was God?" or "Why did God . . . ?" Now you are giving me the chance to answer your questions in the pages of this book.

Table Contents

Foreword

An invitation to journey . . .

No one who lives long enough escapes the journey of tragedy. This reality is as sure as April 15, and that one-day a funeral home will be called on our behalf. How will we journey the treacherous terrain? To be sure those of us who are Christ followers will not grieve as "those who have no hope," but we will grieve! How will we respond when (not if) tragedy comes? Make no mistake tragedy will come! Will you be ready?

You Only Think God Is Silent offers the most compelling, course-correcting map I have encountered to traverse the territory of a tragedy journey. Whether you've made this trip without a map, you are in the midst of a tragedy, or you are reading this in the "pre-need" phase of your life, this book is a must read!

Ten years ago, I first met the author when I came to serve as pastor of the church where she was the part-time music minister. I quickly grew to appreciate the depth of talent and commitment she brought to the ministry. I also rapidly saw her talents for ministry went far beyond the area of music. The only thing that happened more quickly than both of these was my friendship with her and her husband. He was my first fly-fishing instructor and my skeet-shooting buddy. He was also an incredible Sunday school teacher and worship leader. He prayed the most beautiful, eloquent, heart-felt prayers I've ever heard. The author and I shared a deep love for music and one of my greatest sources of joy was singing under her incredible leadership. Through it all, I kept sensing God had bigger plans for her ministry. I began to encourage (she might say push) her to explore other areas of ministry. I saw in her an incredible capacity to communicate the faith articulately. It took some persuasion, but I got her to preach, though she refused to call it preaching! She said we could call it a devotional, or sharing, or teaching, anything but preaching. Semantics aside, be it known by all who read these words, she preached! With this work, her gift for communicating the faith is extended to the written word. It is hard to believe our friendship now extends a decade. Even more incomprehensible to me is that it has been three years since Elan's death. This book has already been of assistance to me as I continue my tragedy journey related to his death.

As I complete the writing of these word's God has given me a remarkable gift in the form of the scripture lesson assigned to read this day in my Transformational Journal devotional. The scripture: I Kings 19. It is the story that has been a refrain echoing in my ears as I've read *You Only Think God Is Silent.* Elijah, the great prophet, in fear, high-tails it to Mount Sinai, the mountain where Moses encountered the burning bush, where the Israelites newly freed from slavery encountered the thunderous theophany of God, that mount from which the commandments were carved. On Sinai, in the midst of the most frightening experience of his life, Elijah encounters the living God. How would God appear? Like he did to Moses? In the wind, earthquake, and fire of his self-revelation to the Israelites? Through carving eternal words into the side of the mountain so that Elijah would never forget? The passage says God was not in any of these tried and true forms of self-revelation; instead, God speaks to Elijah in a gentle whisper. The encounter closes with a transformed Elijah whose fear is traded for faith, whose call is renewed and whose purpose is clear. This clarity and renewal only comes to those who wait and do so in silence and stillness. Shhhh, my fellow tragedy journey traveler, listen! *You Only Think God Is Silent.*

You're invited on a journey. Not a solo journey where you

must make your own way. The invitation is to journey with a seasoned traveler, a sage guide. The road the pages ahead take you down were not garnered through great literature or distilled from the wisdom of the academy, instead they come from the unique learning that it birthed through a journey deep into the valley of the shadow of death, past bitter waters to a place of refreshment, restoration and renewal. Like all journeys worth traveling, there will be hills to climb, rough waters to traverse, obstacles to overcome, but the payoff is a place of beauty, a place of renewal and rest, with breathtaking views that fill us with awe. Ultimately, the journey brings us to a new place, a new home, a promised land.

God is with us! We are not alone! Thanks be to God!

Rev. J. Timothy Jarrell
March 19, 2005

Introduction

For as long as I can remember I could always hear God. Sometimes it was in the wind in the pine trees of the mountains. At other times, it was in the wind as it blew through my hair while I raced around a track on a bicycle. Most of the time it was in the Peace that was unexplainable, and there were those moments when I heard the still, small voice speak clearly to me. However, I had never known God to be silent, until the night of my thirty-eighth birthday, when my husband of almost 14 years did not come home from work. He was never late without calling. As I sat in the kitchen feeding our four-month-old baby and helping our second-grade daughter with her homework, I looked at the clock on the kitchen oven and realized he was late. For a brief moment, I felt God telling me I had become a widow. I did not want to listen, and for the first time in my memory, God seemed to be silent.

In the next hours and then days, we searched for a missing person. Later we found that my husband had been buried alive on a work site, and I experienced a mountain of emotions and activity. First chaos, then a fog of grief and confusion, anger, pain, questions, and then a profound realization—God certainly was not silent!

You Only Think God Is Silent speaks to the difficult question: When the inevitable crises of life occur, will you blame God as the perpetrator of the crisis, or will you see God as the One ready to sustain, provide, and transform you during this time? All of us will experience tragedy in the loss of a loved one, loss of health, loss of relationships, struggles in living with abuse, financial and career challenges, and the list goes on. No one will escape living with pain.

As people of faith, we need to develop a refined and pure

13

understanding of God's will prior to the fire and test of tragedy. We will all experience tragedy. We cannot allow the world or even well-meaning children of God, who have not refined their understanding of God's will, to convince us that evil is God's will. If you have not sought to establish a refined understanding of God's will, this book is an opportunity to do just that. If you have that understanding, this book will affirm it.

We need to realize that a healthy relationship with God is synergistic in nature. The give and take generates a constant growth that will have moments of complete understanding as well as moments of question. We are not puppets on strings; we do have free will. Therefore, we will be struck by the actions of those who exercise their free will to live apart from God's will. Tragedy generates anger and questions. God is not threatened by our anger and questions. God does not turn away from us or desert us. In addition, we must choose to exercise our free will to allow God to sustain us.

We need to look at specific areas where we should expend energy in attempting to grow and become more like what God had in mind when He created us. Defining moments provide the opportunity to examine ourselves so that we can grow as Christians, maturing in our faith. I have seen this occur in the changes in my own self-perception, my definition of friendship, and even in my definition of parenting. Defining moments provide the opportunity to allow God to mature and complete our faith by changing our hearts and empowering us to forgive.

When people look at my life and my circumstances, I do not want them to feel sorry for me or to pity me. Although each time I tell someone I am a widow, the response is "I'm sorry." Rather, I want people to see me and see the miracle God has done in the lives of my children and in my life. I want them to see a living message in us that proclaims—God is good all the time! I want them to see happiness brought forth by God. I want them to see how good God is and what God can do. I want them to marvel at God! God has lifted me out of the muddiest, darkest, most pitiful, and sorrowful place I could have imagined. More than that, God has put a song in my heart. For each one of us, divine, sacred joy is one choice away.

Tragedy will not define us. Rather, our response to tragedy becomes our defining moment. Tragedy can provide the opportunity for God to transform us.

The closer we come to a mature and complete faith, the more boldly we can go where God sends us to complete His work as He leads.

My prayer is that through this book, we will all hear more clearly the voice of God. I pray that we will be able to find courage as we face challenges and strength to overcome the most daunting obstacles. In addition, I pray that we will be mindful that our help, strength, and support come from God.

My Last Birthday

On my thirty-eighth birthday, I sat at my kitchen table feeding my four-month-old son. It had been an ordinary day. The morning was typical, getting our daughter off to school and a sitter settled in with the baby. I was almost late for work, again, and the day was a normal Friday. I was looking forward to going out for dinner to celebrate my birthday. Of course, it would be a child-friendly family dinner, but that was what we always did because that was what we enjoyed most. It was my birthday, but other than a morning birthday serenade from my husband and daughter and a bakery cake sitting on the kitchen counter, it was a typical day. The clock on the stove read 5:50 P.M. My husband, Elan, was late. He said he would be home at 5:30. He was absolutely never late without a phone call. God spoke to my heart and I knew. I clearly remember asking myself, *I'm a widow on my thirty-eighth birthday?* I didn't like the answer that my heart knew, so I quit listening. For the next several days, I truly thought God was silent. Never before had I experienced silence from God. I have now come to understand that God was not silent; I was not listening. All the while, God was very much present, speaking, and at work.

We all encounter tragedy in our lifetimes. No one is immune to heartache and difficulty, but for each one of us, these tragedies become the defining moments of our lives. It is not tragedy that defines us, and we must not make the mistake of allowing the tragedy to define us. Further, the tragedy does not define God. God is not defeated in our struggles. Rather, it is how we respond to tragedy and how we see and listen to God in our times of tragedy and struggle that defines us. Therefore, our response in tragedy becomes our defining moment. Our definition is reliant upon our response as who we are, and more significantly, as Whose we are. We define ourselves as children of faith when we seek God at these moments, and God defines Himself as He sustains us and protects us in these times, regardless of our ability to hear his voice.

After I chose not to listen to God, I did as most of us do and sprung into action. I was going to fix this situation. I called Elan's coworkers and members of the church to see who knew where he was. Elan's good friend was going through a difficult separation, and I convinced myself that he was talking with him and helping him through a hard day. However, when I reached him by phone, he told me that he had not talked to him all day. Elan was a hydrogeologist, and he had been out on a field job collecting soil samples at a construction site. At the close of the day, the track hoe driver, rushing his job, backfilled a trench with concrete slabs and dirt without checking to see if Elan was clear of the trench. Elan was buried alive in the trench. As the track hoe driver left the work site, he realized Elan's truck was still there, open and empty. I will never know what he was thinking, but I do know he just left the site. After several phone calls, Elan's truck was found just as it was left. It was now about nine o'clock at night. Instantly more phone calls were made, first to police and then to more friends. Within a couple of hours, 75 or more men had gathered at the construction site to begin looking for Elan. They were not allowed on the property until the police had finished working the area with a search helicopter and search and rescue dogs. After hours of waiting, the men created a line across the property, and they performed a search on foot. Elan was not found. People gathered at my home to sit with me. My sister rushed to my house to spend the night and to take care of my small children while I went to the construction site to join the search. My thoughts could not have been much different than anyone else's in this type of situation: I convinced myself that I could find him. It would only take me moments, and I would take care of it. I had always fought with the difficulty of self-sufficiency. When I arrived, I began walking the construction site. I did *not* find him quickly. I was questioned by the police as they tried to make sense of things. They asked questions about his mood, our plans that Friday, and my birthday. They also asked questions about our marriage and those questions hurt, but they had to be asked by the police. It took a very short while for the police to understand—this was an amazing and honorable man who loved his wife and children deeply. Everyone involved in the search could tell that he was extraordinary and a devoted, loving husband. His disappearance was confusing and impossible to grasp.

When the questions ended, I walked the property some more. For an instant, I heard God speak, and I listened for that brief moment. I heard "He is not here." I had heard that one other time, and I suddenly remembered, although I did not want to remember. I had been teaching in Southern California at the start of my teaching career. In my fourth year there, one of my students was shot in a drive-by shooting. She took a bullet in the side of her head. She had been transported to a hospital and was put on life support systems, but absolutely no brain waves could be detected. Her mother would not turn off the life support

19

machines until I told her daughter to wake up. She just knew that since her daughter had always done what I had asked, if I asked her to wake up, she would. As I walked into the ICU with her mother, I heard a voice say, "Tell her she is not here." I believe God knew that I would recall and would know, but I did not want to know. I heard the words "He is not here" and quickly chose not to listen. I worked hard for the next several days not to hear God. As I came back to the police cars at the entrance of the construction site, one of the officers met me and informed me that the track hoe driver had seen some men in a white truck take Elan off the property. That was easier to hear than what I knew in my heart God was trying to tell me. I decided that "He is not here" meant that I needed to look for him off the property.

The next day I worked with six search teams of friends and family to search the entire city and outlying area to find Elan. He was not found. The next three days are a painful blur. I know that I continued to search for a missing or abducted person. Hospitals and shelters were checked, I continued to search in abandon buildings and properties near the site, and friends continued to offer rewards for information leading to his recovery. All the while, the police continued to look for a buried man. The testing area was reopened by the same track hoe driver that buried Elan. Days of digging passed slowly, as we continued to plead through the media for help to find a missing person. Every sunset was heartbreaking as it signaled another day without finding him, and through all of these days, I asked myself, "Why is God silent?"

Finally, I stopped. Perhaps it was because I was too tired to keep going in my own direction. Perhaps it was because I knew what God had spoken to my heart six days before was truth, or perhaps I finally wanted to listen more than I wanted to make my own solution. Whatever the reason, I stopped. Then I knew. The next morning Elan's body was recovered.

As I began making funeral plans, the house filled with more food, gifts, cards, plants, relatives, visitors, and chaos. I found comfort in reading every card and letter that arrived. Among all of this, a small book arrived. It is strange. I cannot find it now and don't even remember the title, but one message stood out and changed everything for me. The lesson I learned is that it is understandable not to have the resources to manage the pain or to make sense of the tragedy. The solution is to give the pain to God, along with permission for God to use the situation to be glorified as He wills. I chose God's glorification! At Elan's funeral, more than one thousand people took communion together and heard about how Elan never "got over the cross." They heard of the awe and wonder and tearful thankfulness Elan always had for the cross. God was already receiving glory. The days Elan was missing, the week of the funeral, and the years since have all been used by God to teach me and grow me in ways many people never get a chance to learn and experience.

Most important among those lessons was an affirmation of my faith. Nothing that happened during all of this has been inconsistent with my faith, my theology, or my understanding of God. Although I spent several days thinking God was silent, I am certain that God was never silent!

Psalm 37:5–6 "Commit your way to the Lord; trust in him and he will do this: He will make your righteousness shine like the dawn, the justice of your cause like the noonday sun." NIV

Forecast-
Crisis of Faith

Right away chaos set in. Media descended on the area where Elan's truck was found. The site resembled a flea market, and this is where I spent every hour of daylight for the week we searched. A family support trailer was parked on the site. Another trailer served as a meeting place for the police. Elan's co-workers watched carefully as the testing trenches were re-opened. Other coworkers set up sandwiches and soft drinks in pickup trucks for those helping. Media was confined to a designated area, and I tried to keep my distance from them. Camera lenses seemed to constantly point in my direction. A second track hoe was moved onto the site to help dig. Aerial photos were taken, and I studied them as if I could find him in them. Helicopters hovered overhead making a constant noise that blended with the heavy equipment engines and the reverse warning beeping of those machines. Friends from church and work sat with me as I watched helplessly. I felt so lost. Every time a track hoe would stop digging, my heart would stop. I just knew they stopped because they found him. In those seconds, I would lose all hope of ever seeing my husband again. Then the digging would start again, and my heart would also start again. My ability to re-ignite the hope of finding my husband alive was not as quick as those engines though. The emotional rollercoaster was intolerable. The police would update me with any information or ideas they had. I remember one meeting in a police trailer where the anxiety became so overwhelming I could not breathe. I simply didn't know what to do. The first few days I would search abandoned properties nearby and walk through creek beds and any possible location where Elan may have been.

The media watched my every move, looking for additions to the story of a missing man that made no sense. I resorted to sitting and hiding in a hedgerow that ran along the side of the construction site property. There I could sit and watch as the digging continued without interruption from the media or onlookers. It seemed as though I gained some sort of privacy there. When the sun would set and the search efforts would cease until the next day, I would go home. My house was filled with family and friends to comfort and help. My sister sat with my daughter to do homework, my mother took care of my baby, and three friends worked around the clock keeping the house organized. Food, cards, calls, and demonstrations of support flooded the house. These ladies sorted, recorded, and managed it all, including feeding everyone meals and keeping the house clean.

The phone rang constantly, and every time it rang, my heart stopped. I wanted it to be Elan calling. The doorbell rang repeatedly, and each time I would jump, knowing it was Elan having made his way home. I began to suffer incredible fatigue and stress, and so visitors began to be screened, but it was still constant chaos.

After Elan's body was recovered at the construction site in the exact location of the sample he was taking, and the funeral planning began—a surreal fog set in. The entire day would pass without any clear thoughts or even memories of them now. I felt numb, I could not sleep, and I don't remember eating. I felt like I was watching my life as it happened as a spectator. I remember watching the press conference where I spoke about finding his body on the news. It seemed bizarre, and that feeling did not leave me after the television was shut off. So much of that time is a blur in my memory. Despite the thick fog, one conversation stands out clearly.

A pastor–undoubtedly trying to help–made a prediction. He forecast an incoming crisis of faith. He told me of a difficulty he was certain I would have–anger with God and doubt about my faith. This forecast seemed strange to me. Those feelings toward God are not unusual, but I had never experienced them. They did not fit within the spectrum of my faith and who I knew God to be. Equally as strange were many of the comments made about this all being God's will or some kind of test. Those comments would strike me and ring through the fog like a foghorn. Each time I would know in my heart that this was not a test or a twisted part of God's will. That was not consistent with my faith and who I knew God to be. Through the chaos of Elan missing and the funeral planning, I lived in a dense fog filled with confusion. With one exception, I was not confused about whether or not this was a test or a part of God's plan.

The forecast of a crisis of faith turned out to be erroneous. I never had the crisis, and I never had anger toward God. It's not because I am super-human or in some way above it. On the contrary, I am no different from any other person who hurts. I can now say, years later, it is because of an exercised and developed faith. The crisis of faith did not arrive because nothing that has happened or is happening is inconsistent with the faith I possess and the God I know. While many forecast a crisis of faith at the onset of tragedy, it is not required. I endured a chaotic, senseless, unexpected tragedy. I was no more prepared for it than anyone would be, with one exception; I possessed an exercised and developed faith. Even though I could not seem to hear God during the height of the chaos, in my heart I knew that I had not passed through that time alone. God was sustaining and caring for me from the moment I was left a widow. How can that lead to a crisis of faith?

Not everyone has the blessing of entering into tragedy with an exercised and developed faith. Not everyone realizes that at some point tragedy must be faced. The reality is that we will face tragedy, and we need a faith that will not shift into crisis mode when it hits. Wherever you are in your journey, it is not too late to gain faith, exercise and grow that faith, and develop that faith into a means to call out to God in the tragedies of life. God is not silent and has not left you.

Hebrews 13:5 "I will never leave you, or forsake you."
NRSV

Faith Is Like A Car

I was a small child, probably six or seven years old, when I learned how important it is to maintain your car. Most significantly, this is also when I learned why your car is like your faith. Most children spend their time in church trying to fight boredom without getting in trouble. I was no different. I can remember some Sundays in my early elementary school years practicing my counting skills by counting how many words were in the closing hymn. Later as my math skills improved, I practiced dividing by counting the words and finding the exact middle of the hymn—all the while trying to sit still enough to make my parents think I was paying attention.

Something was happening though, whether I was paying attention or not. In all that word counting, I grew to love the great old hymns. Amid the feigned attention, I learned many truths about faith from one of the finest storytellers and teachers ever to fill a pulpit. While I may have started counting words in hymns, I ended with the sum of a strong faith foundation.

One Sunday's lesson is still as vivid today as when I heard it as a child. Reverend Don Ian Smith was teaching us all about automobile maintenance, and this particular topic captured my childish attention. As he discussed regular oil changes and attention to fluid levels, I became more and more attentive and curious. My father always maintained our cars at home, and I was taken that others would follow the same practice. I was still young enough to think that my father was the only man-hero out there. I believed that my dad was unique in his ability to work all day at the office and come home to change the oil or mow the yard with amazing, flawless, perfection. Captured by the topic and the way it related to my home, I listened carefully. Reverend Don Smith explained clearly that you maintain your car for many obvious reasons, but the most important reason is not thought of often. The most important reason to carefully maintain your car is for emergencies. If you need your car for transportation in an emergency, you can get in and go! You don't want to be rushing toward your car wondering if it will work. I sat there thankful that I had seen my daddy working on the cars often and confident that they were well maintained. Then Reverend Smith made the crucial connection. "Your faith is like that car." It must be maintained and tuned so that you know when the emergency comes, you have a faith that will carry you through.

I was young and I did not completely understand, but that lesson stuck with me. As I grew, my parents maintained my faith for me until I was old enough to do it myself. I was in church every Sunday. I was sent to Bible school and Sunday school at every opportunity. Gradually, I began caring for my faith myself. I don't know how old I was when I quit counting words in the hymns and dividing to find the middle. At some point, the lessons of Reverend Don Ian Smith became my focus. I took on the task of faith tune-ups. I recall in seventh grade, beginning to engage in daily devotional time. That was facilitated by early years of Bible reading and learning. Over years of attention, my faith became a working vehicle, still requiring consistent, purposeful attention. Through guidance from my parents, excellent teaching from Sunday school teachers, and my own devotional study and reading, I developed a faith that was like the kind of car you can count on in an emergency.

Testing my faith and tuning it up started in my early teen years, while struggling to fit in and suffering the typical teasing of early teens. I was forced to assess the needs my faith could meet, and relied on faith during the days when I dealt with my best friend dumping me to be in the popular crowd. I sacrificed time, energy, and popularity to pay for and acquire the faith I needed. I held true to my faith as I avoided the student parties of high school and again suffered blows to my ability to fit in and be accepted. I continued the work of strengthening and maintaining my faith. Sometimes I did it well and other times not as well. The fact is—the maintenance and development program is continual. Just as the car must continually be maintained, owning your faith simply means you are on a continual maintenance plan.

Faith acquisition is a lot like buying a good car—assess your needs, pay the price, acquire the vehicle, and maintain it constantly. Too many people will do this for a car, but never take the time to do it for their soul. A car must work in all conditions and all situations–good or bad, warm weather or cold, storms or sunshine, going uphill or down, rugged roads or paved. Your faith is exactly the same, because you will encounter it all. The needs you will have will include all the kinds the human experience has to offer—good and bad, warm and cold, storms and sunshine, rough roads and smooth. It is critically important that you make the decision to pay the price to acquire the faith that meets those needs, and then maintain it and strengthen it.

I am always grateful to Reverend Don Ian Smith for teaching me at a very early age to connect this analogy to my faith. In my life, as in any life, I have had all weather and all terrain needs. When I left for college, I found myself sitting on an airplane going to attend school on a campus I had never seen, 2,000 miles from home, so I prayed! I went to that college on an act of faith–the entire plane trip was spent in prayer over my unknown roommate. It turned out that while I was praying, Pam's room arrangements were suddenly, inexplicably changed, and she was moved to a different dorm and a new room. Pam became my roommate and is still my dearest friend. My faith gave me the courage to go to that college, the confidence to ask God for what I needed, and the peace to know it was in his hands.

Faith that is maintained can help a college student know what to pray for and give confidence to a graduate student who is trying to finish a seemingly impossible degree. Faith that is maintained helps you know your calling and purpose because you are equipped to submit to God's leading and calling instead of a worldly demand and set of priorities.

My faith enabled God to lead me into teaching and into my first teaching job in inner city Southern California, where I was blessed to be part of some amazing work. An acquired faith that is rugged enough for the terrain of life and maintained well enough to handle the demands of life can transport you through the dark valleys and allow you to see all the bright mountain tops that God has in store as you travel this life.

The most exciting part of the journey is that God will be present through it all. God will use the travels to strengthen and mature your faith further. When your faith is in good working order, the rough roads can be traveled and God's goodness can be seen even in the darkest valleys. A working faith is more than insurance against hell–it is assurance for the living of life today.

Psalm 23:4 Yea, though I walk through the valley of the shadow of death, I will fear no evil: for thou art with me; thy rod and thy staff, they comfort me. KJV

A Faith That Weathers The Storm

I found myself sitting in an intensive care unit saying good-bye to a student who had been shot; it was tragic. The nightmares and tears that followed her funeral were a struggle. Working while in college when those around me did not "need" to work was difficult. Carrying my infant in his car seat into his daddy's funeral while clutching my young daughter's hand—that was a crisis. A faith that weathers the storm has, at the core, an answer to a profound question: Do you see the tragedies, difficulties, struggles, and crises of your life as perpetrated by God, or do you see God's role as the One ready to transform you and sustain you in these times?

A faith that weathers the storm starts with an all-purpose faith that can handle any size storm. We don't need to board up our windows for a light rain. In addition, we should never face a hurricane with only an umbrella. Too often people respond to a light rain in their lives with boarded windows, as though it were a tragedy or a crisis. When real tragedy comes, these people lack the perspective to deal with it. Those who overreact are often the first to blame God in times of true crisis. We are responsible for recognizing what we are enduring as either a struggle or a crisis. As we exercise faith to endure, we become better equipped and more mature in our faith. As we exercise our faith, we must be certain that it is strong, consistent, and prepared for all types of difficulties, struggles, tragedies, and crises. We must build a multifaceted faith that is equipped to handle every aspect of life from joy to tears.

A faith that weathers storms starts at recognizing the differences between our experiences of difficulty and crises and then requires recognition of our God as God and the part God plays in those experiences. We must answer that profound and fundamental question: Is tragedy something God perpetrates upon us, or is it God's role to sustain us and strengthen us? The answer is crucial. A faith that is consistent, a faith that works, must be able to recognize the source of tragedy and crises. Then, and most importantly, that faith leads us to know the source of strength to endure all difficulties.

During the time immediately after my husband's death and in the years since, I have heard many semi-theological platitudes that if believed would lead to a crisis of faith. Honestly, I believe these were presented as an attempt to comfort or as an offering when a well-meaning person simply did not know what to say. Regardless, to endure the tragedy without a crisis of faith requires an answer that is consistent with Scripture and understandable on the heart level.

I will not accept the semi-theological platitudes that God made my husband's death happen—that it was "just God's plan for it to be his time." Nor will I accept in some way that it was God's punishment of my children or me. These faith statements are inconsistent with Scripture and are the ideal foundations for a crisis of faith and a deep anger with God.

I have been blessed with opportunities in my life prior to Elan's death that provided the proving ground for my faith convictions. If we watch for these opportunities to exercise our faith, we will see that all of us have the chance to develop and prove our faith convictions and bring them to a heart level. My faith convictions have been unshaken by all that I have experienced. Rather, the experiences have proven them and solidified them in my heart.

I believe in my heart that God is omnipotent–God is all-powerful. God has not used that power to create a world of stringed puppets. On the contrary, God utilized His incomprehensible power to take the incomprehensible action and to give all created humanity free will. God acted so that the amazing relationship we can have is not diminished by obligation. Rather, our relationship with God is enhanced by the freedom to choose it. God will not force you into a relationship; you must choose it. God will not make the choice for you; you must choose it. God will seek you, pursue you, reach for you—but you must also choose the relationship with God.

This element of free will has been difficult for humanity from the earliest scriptural accounts. Genesis tells us we chose evil. We live in a fallen condition. People choose to ignore and even reject God. Throughout Scripture, we see these choices made. One chooses God, another does not; righteousness and evil co-exist. We do not live in the garden. Our world is not perfect and disease occurs. People choose to reject God and go their own way and tragedy happens. The forces of the world in which we live generate natural disasters. Our beliefs are inconsistent with the grace and redeeming power of the cross of Jesus when we determine that God perpetrates these products of evil upon us. God is omnipotent and powerful enough to allow us free will. When we choose the relationship with God, then we see the role God plays in our struggles, tragedies, and crises. When we choose God, we are sustained through the difficulties, tragedies, and crises we will encounter.

Let me specifically explain how this is consistent with what I have lived. A man working on a track hoe did not take the necessary precautions on Friday afternoon. He rushed. He wasn't vigilant with honor and care in his work. He buried my husband alive. That was not God's will. That was the will of a human. God's will was manifest in the innumerable ways that my family and I were sustained and in the way every need has been and continues to be met. To be sustained, even into eternity, is God's will. It was not God's will that Elan was buried. The moment he was, God's role became all-important as Elan was delivered into eternity. That is God's will.

God is omniscient–God is all knowing. God will speak to us by the Holy Spirit, through others around us who are listening, and through peace. God knows, but that doesn't mean we will listen and respond to the guidance given. How many times have you been urged from within or from others to change direction or plans only to find you averted disaster? I do believe that God knew what was to happen that afternoon. I can see places where God spoke to me and to Elan and put in place many provisions before the day. Once again, we are not puppets on a string. I will never know what Elan felt before he went to take his last water sample. Did he have a feeling, an urging not to go? Someday I will get to ask him, but on that glorious day, I doubt it will even cross my mind.

God is omnipresent. God will not leave us. He is present to comfort, guide, and sustain.

Matthew 28:20 "And remember, I am with you always, to the end of the age." NRSV

If we want a faith that works, one that weathers the storms, we must start at the place where we recognize what is God's will and what comes from God. We cannot settle for semi-theological platitudes or beliefs that are inconsistent with Scripture. We must go further and sort through the shortcut answers to a truth that stands the test of life experience. All good and perfect things come from God. That does not mean that all we experience is generated by God. Far from it! We will encounter the effects of living in a fallen world.

Next, we must develop the ability to see the hand of God, as we are sustained and uplifted. God reaches out to you and will carry you, lead you, and protect you, but you must choose to let Him. God's sustaining hand was visible to me in the very first hours of losing my husband as people arrived at my home to sit with me and watch my children. God's sustaining hand was seen in those who would search through the night and into the coming days. God's hand was apparent in people prompted to provide plane tickets for my parents to fly in and be with me. Others were prompted to open homes to provide places to stay for Elan's parents and the many extended family members who eventually arrived. God's hand was everywhere I looked.

Finally, you must definitively answer for yourself this question: Will you see tragedy as something God has perpetrated upon you—or as something through which God wants to sustain you?

Romans 8:38–39 "For I am convinced that neither death, nor life, nor angels, nor rulers, nor things present, nor things to come, nor powers, nor height, nor depth, nor anything else in all creation, will be able to separate us from the love of God in Christ Jesus our Lord." NRSV

For I Know The Plans
I Have For You

Four months after Elan's death, she approached me at church with an apologetic tone. More than a year before Jane had promised she would not sell her last piece of land without giving Elan and I a chance to buy it first. Now she needed to sell it, and the timing seemed horrible. Yet Jane was keeping her word. I responded quickly, "I can't do that now." Then I stopped, "Let me pray about it before I make a decision." I had a difficult decision to make. I had dreamed with my husband about owning that land and building a house there. Now facing life without a husband and with two small children who completely depended on me, the decision seemed clear. I should give up on the dream of living on that land. I knew I could not handle the addition of land to the list of demands in my life. Before I made a decision, though, I knew I had to pray and seek God's direction. Praying first then deciding was becoming more common now than in my past.

I prayed. I heard an answer in Jeremiah 29:11 *"For surely I know the plans I have for you, says the Lord, plans for your welfare and not for harm, to give you a future with hope."* NRSV Two truths became clear. God was not through with me; there were plans for hope and a future, and I knew I should buy the land. A thorough reading of the Old Testament reveals that from the instant Eve chose the apple, from the moment of the fall, God began restoration. God set into motion a plan that eventually culminated with the ultimate act of Grace at Calvary. Humanity chose evil–God chose to move toward reconciliation. Along the way, there were many steps. God used prophets, floods, covenants, and the freeing of an entire nation. God gave a law to establish an understandable process of sacrifice for forgiveness, and then God provided the total sacrifice and forgave us all, thereby reconciling us to God.

God's reconstruction of the human condition was in place before we knew our need. The moment evil was chosen in the Garden, the cross on Calvary, as part of the plan of restoration, came into view in the distance. My experience with tragedy is consistent with this. The moment the track hoe driver chose to rush and do the dishonorable in hiding cement that should have been hauled away–at the moment his evil touched my family's life–at the moment the cement buried my husband–God's plan for restoration began to shine on the horizon–and He has sustained me and carried me through as I journey toward it.

As I started on the journey, I felt God's hand literally cradle me and carry me. God has a plan for me and wants me to have a future, so God began transforming me. Slowly, piece by piece, the shattered shards of the picture window that once was my life were placed into a new stained glass picture by God's hand.

As with anyone who experiences loss can attest, some of my friends could not cope with the pain. Many of them simply could not grasp that my grief outlasted their patience. Others simply could not cope with the pain they felt at the reality of my life. Nearly all my friendships dissolved. Further, situations that once were commonplace didn't fit anymore. The destruction seemed to continue to ripple without limit. Even coaching my daughter's soccer team came apart. I knew I had to take a leave from my church job, which eventually led to resigning that position, and ultimately leaving that church. One piece after another continued to fall out of the old window frame as God carefully reconstructed the new picture. With each piece that no longer fit, I continued to wonder how God could manage any restoration. Slowly, God put enough of the pieces into place, and I could see a new picture beginning to form.

One key piece of the picture was my teaching. God transformed my perspective, and I became aware that the lesson I was to teach had more emphasis on living out what God was doing to sustain me and less to do with subject matter or winning scores received at contests. I became aware of living a testimony instead of only speaking it.

New and vital friendships were formed with people who had suffered loss or who simply had an amazing compassion and care. A group of women pulled together to make certain my workday childcare needs were met. Men in the church came together to ensure that my house maintenance needs were met. High school students set up a calendar to meet my childcare needs so I could continue my one hobby of playing soccer. Neighbors helped with grocery shopping. A nearby church arranged for meals to be cooked and brought to my home for three months while I tried to gather myself together to teach. A grief counselor made herself available to my children and to me at no cost so we could have guidance in the healing process. Elan's boss set up a variety of assistance needed to help me keep up with the maintenance and care of our lawn and home.

God's hand of provision could be seen in every aspect of my life. There was an amazing clarity each time a decision needed to be made. The Holy Spirit blessed me with an infusion of guidance. The clarity of guidance came paired with an overwhelming sense of peace. While all of this is amazing, the most remarkable was the restoration process God worked on in my heart. A transformation began. I was put into a situation that made me examine personality traits and habits that were not healthy for my relationship with God or for me. One of the traits I have already mentioned is a 'prayer first' mentality. I had become accustomed, like many of us, to making most minor decisions on my own and calling on God for the bigger ones. Now in a totally broken state, I relied on God for the smallest to the largest and all decisions in between. I submitted myself in full surrender to Him like I never had before–not out of wisdom–but because I was so broken I had no other option. God had something in mind when He created me, just as He did with all of us. During this tragedy, He has used the opportunity of my broken state and depth of submission to move me closer to what He had in mind when He created me.

For the first time in my life, I was totally dependent on God. Matthew 6:25–34 tells us we do not have to worry about what to eat or what to wear. I LIVED that! Literally! Each day I would walk into my very full closet—and honestly–only one outfit would seem in focus. I would wear it to find that it was exactly right for the day—a pantsuit the day I unexpectedly had to set up a stage for an assembly the next day, a cool outfit the day the air conditioner malfunctioned in my classroom, a skirt and suit coat the day the superintendent dropped in to let me know he was thinking of me. God guided the small decisions, like clothing, and the very important decisions like starting grief counseling for my children and me right away. I was transformed into a person who found abundant joy in submission to God.

The transformation made me look at my self-esteem and reassess some of my hyper, self-critical practices. God had empowered me to let go of some bits of my personality I didn't even realize were so much a part of me, like my self-consciousness or my need to be in control. This transformation continues because I can only deal with traits of which I am aware. As God carries me through one area and transforms me, another is revealed. As I continue, I become closer to God and even more filled with the abundant joy that Jesus tells us about.

Another transformation is in my willingness to tell others of God's goodness, even to write it down. This has not been an easy road. I have had to look at parts of myself I probably never would have examined, and I have been led to make decisions that have been difficult and painful. I have lived and learned that in tragedy and struggle God's desire is not to give us what we want; rather, it is to transform us and give us what we need. I have had to release to God many friendships and relationships; I was led to resign my position as the music minister at my church. These are hard decisions, but I know God is leading me to His restoration and my transformation, so I will continue to follow. I know God will continue to lead. He has plans to give me a future with hope–and He will lead me! Nevertheless, my prayers cannot be for a quick fix or an easy out of the struggle and rough times. I must pray for transformation and change so I can navigate the rough times. What God knows I need is transformation, not indulgence. I must trust God and receive what I need, not concerning myself with the easy fix we all too often want.

I firmly believe that God did not will the tragedy in my life. God's will has been to sustain me through this time, transform me, and to guide me into a restored life. I have not been alone, not even for an instant. God has been a real presence

The Man Named Job

The school pep rally ended and the students were being released. I stood in the stands like many other teachers supervising the students as they filed out. Then I heard her cheerful and familiar voice, "Mrs. Allen!" In only a few days, her son would leave my class at the end of his middle school years and head off to high school. Over the past three years, she and I had become well acquainted. We talked about her son, how he was progressing, and of course, looking forward to high school. Then she asked about me. She had been there with me, as many other parents of students in her son's class, through it all. These students celebrated the birth of my second child and wept with me at my husband's funeral, while only in their sixth-grade year of school. They stuck with me as tolerant students during grade 7 when I endured my first year as a widow, with more down days than up. Now as I am beginning to stand up again, they are growing up and going on to high school. This mom knows what she is asking when she asks about how I am doing. In the course of our conversation, she tells me that when God restores my life and me, although it is hard to imagine, it will be better than ever. "You may not believe me!" she laughs. As sincerely as I can, I tell her, "I believe you. The book of Job says I should."

The book of Job—now that is one to which I can relate. Within a nine-month period, I lost my husband, my grandmother who I was very close to, and my very well loved dog of 14 years. My brother and sister-in-law lost a baby, and my sister and brother-in-law dealt with the horrible disappointment of infertility and failed adoption attempts. Additionally, there were many lost friendships, a lost church position, and even the end to coaching my daughter's soccer team. It really seemed like everything was being stripped away, and all of my family was grieving and surrounded with sorrow. To keep myself from complete self-pity, I would joke. When people asked about my life, I would tell them I was looking into having my name legally changed to Job. The truth was–and is–there is so much to learn from the book of Job.

Job had a great life. He was wealthy and revered God. He had a wonderful family and all a man could want. He attributed all of his good to the hand of God. Then evil attacked, and Job lost all of his livestock and business holdings, his servants were killed, and in a final horrifying hit—his children were killed. While still grieving, disease set in. Even his wife encouraged him to curse God and die. The story is one that strikes at your heart as you read of the inconceivable anguish this one person endures. It is a difficult book to read.

As difficult as it is to read, we must, because we learn many unshakable lessons from Job's responses. First, in his mourning, Job does not charge God with wrongdoing. Second, when even his friends try to convince him that his suffering is some sort of retribution from God, Job does not agree. This is an important, even vital, point for today's Christians. We cannot indulge in the simplistic doctrine of retribution—that we suffer as a punishment or as a warning. This inaccurate attempt to place human understanding and order onto God only adds to the suffering of those struggling with tragedy.

While Job disagrees with his friends, we learn a third lesson. Job doesn't quickly dismiss the comments of his friends. He examines the statements and takes the opportunity to put his beliefs through the refiner's fire. What emerges is a stronger, more resolute set of beliefs. Job clearly defines and solidifies his belief that his tragedies are not retribution.

The fourth lesson is a pivotal one. Job, with resolve in place, directs his questions and grief to God. Job questions God. Job is angry with God, and a great revelation is provided for us–God is there! God is right there with Job in his suffering, questioning, and even Job's anger.

The fifth and probably most difficult lesson comes in Job's exchanges with God. During these times, it becomes clear that we as humans do not have the capacity to understand God fully. We cannot make God fit into finite human logic and reason. We see Job accept God on God's terms, and we learn that we too must accept God as God of the universe, far beyond human reason and ordering. God is God, and God is with us always. In the end, God restores Job's life to even better than before.

I didn't actually try to change my name to Job, but I can tell you that I have experienced the lessons of Job in my life and claim the hope of restoration. The experiences of the past years have reinforced the messages of Job's story. The initial message is the least comforting and the hardest for me to accept: Tragedy happens to all of us. Belief or unbelief, righteous or unrighteous, we all will experience struggles, difficulties, and even tragedies. Further, there will not be clean, easy explanations. Often there are no explanations. This was Job's situation. His closest friends tried to convince him otherwise, but Job soundly rejected the simplistic doctrine of retribution. We must do the same.

There were many priceless and amazed expressions at my response when well-meaning friends would say things like "It was

God's plan" or "God must have wanted Elan now" or "Well, you must know it was God's will." My response? "No, this was not God's will; it was the will of a track hoe driver in a hurry." Job teaches us clearly that we all encounter crisis and tragedy, and we are incapable of putting cause and effect order on these struggles. Job rattles us out of our simplistic misconceptions of God and retribution. No, we are not going to be shaken and suddenly gain clean, clear answers packaged in a nice neat formula. We will be afforded a deeper and more genuine examination of who God is and how we respond to that view of God.

This leads to another lesson from Job that I encountered. People will say the most absurd things, usually as a result of an intense desire to help and a lack of knowing how. I experienced what Job teaches in this area. The reaction to these statements always produced a refining of my convictions and deeply held theological understandings. Through these encounters, my beliefs were tested and my faith was strengthened. Like Job, who in his discussions with his friends gained resolve and strength, I also benefited from these exchanges.

One encounter stands out in my memory, when a close friend came over to my home and said nothing. Amid the chaos, planning, noise, and absurd statements, she entered my family room, sat beside me on my couch, and cried. She cried with me and said nothing. Eventually, she rose, gave me a sincere and agape filled hug and left. For seven days Job's friends did the right thing, they sat in silence and allowed their presence to console him. When my friend left, I felt peace and comfort. I can only presume that Job gained the same from the presence of his friends, until they spoke. When people I love struggle, I try to act on this lesson: Be present; say as little as possible. While the well-intentioned friends with absurd platitudes generated refined and strengthened faith convictions, they also added to my struggle and the intensity of my pain.

After answering to his friends, Job gained enough conviction in his faith that he was willing to take his case to God. I had and still have questions for God. "How am I going to raise two children without a dad? How can I teach my children what a godly man is without their godly father to show them?" Then there were the questions that were more cries of anguish at two in the morning, "How can I do all of the parenting totally alone? Who cares what kind of day I had?" The questions have no limit.

While some have answers, many only have the answer of "Be still, and know that I am God!" Not as lengthy a response as Job received, but certainly similar in the message. The answers have a primary constant—a sense of peace and an understanding that God, the God of the universe, is guiding and caring for me. I do not have to understand.

The refining of beliefs and the strengthening of faith convictions gives the foundation on which to stand and address God. As Job questions God, we learn that God is there with Job. In Job's fortune and tragedy, God is there. In Job's patience and anger, God is there. God accepts Job at both ends of the spectrum. God is always present. In our darkest most tragic moments, when all of the distractions have been destroyed and all that is left is our broken selves and our intense need—that is when the comforting hand of God is easiest to feel. I have felt the amazing power of God lift me and carry me through the darkest days, just as clearly and as real as Job heard God's voice! Tribulation does not indicate an absence of God. God is with us, and we are only alone if we choose to reject God.

The question and answer time between Job and God changed Job, and in the end, he was a humbled and different man. Living these past years, totally reliant on God and with no "answers" in hand, has changed me greatly. No one goes through tragedy unchanged. Further, no one goes through tragedy carried by God and remains the same as an individual or as a faithful believer and disciple. God transforms us and matures us in these times. Job started out as a righteous man, yet his encounter with God in the face of tragedy transformed him and matured him into more than he was before. This can happen for each of us if we take ourselves into God's presence in times of tragedy.

An encounter with God changes a person, even a faithful person. Many faithful Christians have an amazing intellectual faith, yet have not allowed that faith to permeate their hearts. Tragedy brings us to no other choice. It is a fair and reasonable speculation that without his tribulation, Job would never have ventured into God's presence as he did during those tragic times. At the start of the book, Job cognitively knew God. By the end, he experientially knew God. We live this constant faith maturation process. This is the journey of moving deeper and deeper into an experiential knowledge of God. We can experience the joy of accepting God as God, on God's own terms without our human limitations, categorizations, or organizational orderings of God's ways. As part of the wisdom literature in Scripture, the book of Job seeks to order the ways of God. In the end, it helps each of us know that human thinking cannot place order on the ways of God.

God is God, and we don't understand all that means. Acceptance of that brings freedom and joy. The freedom it brings is the freedom to embrace the gracious gift of life and the moment we have in the present. We have been given the gift of life to enjoy freely! The joy is in the embracing of the life we are blessed with, without having to place human ordering or rankings on it. God is God, and we are His children! The mysteries of the universe, as demonstrated in the question to Job, "Where were you when I laid the foundations of the universe?" are beyond us. We are free to accept that truth. Further, Job's survival and restoration proves that we can question, and God is not angered by questions. God demonstrates an acceptance of us as human, with anger, questions, and grief as well as with joy and praise. God created us, God knows us, and God knows that these are all a part of the human condition. God accepts us. We are to accept God, as God. This is demonstrated in that Job does not get clear answers from God. Yet what Job does gain is an understanding of God that many never are able to realize. Perhaps it takes enduring a tragedy to come to this place with God. Like Job, I have come to understand that God is with me in my tears, God hears my questions, and God knows the answers to the questions I ask, as well as knowing what questions I should have asked. God's presence is real, and for that I am exceedingly thankful. We want clear reasons for the difficult situations in life. We see in Job and our own experiences that those clear reasons are not available to those who seek God's truths.

Therefore, I stood there in the gymnasium, and I looked at this mother who had just said, "I know you may not believe it, but someday your life will be better than it ever was."

I sincerely replied, "I do believe it!" Job questioned God, but Job stuck with God, and in the end, Job's life was restored.

No matter what happens, I have learned that I must always keep a childlike faith knowing the most important thing–God is God, and I am not alone.

Job 42:16–17 "After this Job lived a hundred and forty years; he saw his children and their children to the fourth generation, And so he died old and full of years." NIV

A Dynamic Theology

Loneliness is not the absence of people. I have been intensely lonely in crowded rooms. Loneliness is the absence of being known, and knowing.

My marriage was good! It was good because we had invested time and energy into truly knowing each other. My husband knew what kind of day I was having by the clothing I put on after work. I knew his mood by the amount of time it took for him to get from his truck to inside the house after work. Fourteen years of open, honest communication–not just talking, but also listening as well as studying to learn each other's cues had taught us a lot about each other. Things were not perfect, but we always made time to learn about each other and grow. It was a very good marriage. At the time of my husband's death, it was still growing and dynamic.

Any healthy relationship is just that—growing and dynamic. More than anything, you should seek that kind of relationship with God. We are willing to work at a friendship or a romantic relationship. Yet too often, our relationship with God is put on the bottom of the priority list or on the back burner, or it is given a surface polish. Attend the right services and say the right phrases, but keep it on the surface, and don't allow it to generate a total change from the heart.

God wants more for us, and we should too. God wants to

be invited in and to be known. Throughout Scripture, God sets in motion ways for our relationship with Him to be furthered, and he reveals Himself to us in many ways. Yet we fail to connect–to make the relationship a heart relationship–to allow it to define us from the heart. It is this connecting that is crucial for a real, heart-transforming relationship. We can't have an intellectual connection and call it enough. Just like any relationship, we need to be intentional about growing and maturing in our relationship with God. We are to seek that more than anything else, yet many seldom do.

To seek that growing, dynamic, heart-connected relationship with God starts with confronting our need to avoid a completely intellectual pursuit of God without the heart connection. We can see many people like the Pharisees in our churches today. They know the rules. They study, participate, and comply with the rules, but their hearts are untouched. They can handle the theological debates, but their hearts are not on fire. The issue is not to develop a doctoral-level theology. What is required is not an educated theological premise or theory. What is essential is a refined, working, practiced, and dynamic faith and theological understanding that produces a relationship with God that is heart deep. That relationship is so heart deep that it moves you to action in acts of genuine compassion. A heart-deep relationship is one that is working and practiced so that it lifts you in times of crisis. A heart deep faith is practiced and dynamic enough to sustain and direct you as you navigate the dark valleys of real life and living in this world. If this is a faith you already possess, then you know you must continually maintain it so that it remains dynamic. If it is a faith you have yet to experience, then begin to define and refine a theology that is consistent with Scripture and allows God to move in your heart and take your faith genuinely heart deep. Allow God to move within you. We cannot be people of heartfelt love, compassion, and real Christian action without a heart-deep faith. We cannot be faith-filled people who can endure the inevitable crises and tragedies of this life without allowing God to move in our hearts because of a heart-deep faith. My prayer is that each of us will find and develop a heart-deep faith to sustain us through the inevitable tragedies of life.

Get to know God and constantly seek to know God more. Develop a theology that is consistent with Scripture. Study, read, and know God's Word. It is not enough to listen to what another person tells you is found in Scripture. Read it. Read the entire Bible. Then study it! Not just a verse here or there out of context, but do serious study that involves learning the history and setting of each book of Scripture. Study the context—that is the audience the book is written for and the issues it is to address. Allow Scripture to answer questions about Scripture. There are so many resources for this: church-based study groups, civic Bible study groups, resources in Bible commentaries, and good study Bibles. Know God by knowing His Word! Be desperate for Scripture. Know it so that it comes to you naturally in times of need. Knowing God's Word has solidified the foundation of my faith and sustained me in many times of need.

Communication is a key element in any dynamic, healthy relationship. Communicate with God in prayer. Make prayer as common and natural as breathing. Many books are written about prayer, seminars are given, and prayer group meetings are available. If you are in doubt, avail yourself of any of these tools. Do whatever you need to so that the communication is open between you and God. Pray without ceasing. Realize that part of prayer communication is to be still and silent–and listen! Constantly bathe your days in prayer, and listen for God's leading. Practice taking time to be still and silent. Really listen for the response of God.

God leads you with Scripture, and when you listen, God can lead you in response to prayer. Hearing God also involves getting to know God as He is revealed in his servants. Establish solid relationships with others who can and will hold you accountable for your diligence in maintaining and maturing your relationship with God. Accountability is hard, uncomfortable, enriching, and nourishing. Find others who will help you and support you as you strive for a dynamic and growing relationship. If your support is not in your home, seek out a friend or group that can support you. I had that support from my husband. Now I must actively seek friendships that can provide faith support as well as fellowship. We all need to be held accountable. God gives us the ability to live each day in relationship with Him and grow in the depth of that relationship every day. When our theology is defined, refined, practiced, and dynamic, we are prepared to turn to God for guidance daily and in our most desperate and dark hours.

As the time since my husband's death has passed, my faith has carried me when I was too frail to move on my own, and I have experienced clear guidance from God in all these ways. I am thankful that prior to Elan's death, I participated in numerous Bible studies. My understanding of God's revelation of God through Scripture produced a base for comfort and guidance. Scripture answered my questions about my hope and my future in Jeremiah 29:11. Scripture guided my reaction to those who gave questionable opinions and comments by studying Job's three friends. Paul's lessons on peace and contentment in all situations became a determining factor in my attitude.

Prayer had always been natural, but now I cried out to God with an earnest heart, as I never had before. I experienced an uplifting from the prayers of others, which was new. Many comments came to me about how strong or articulate I appeared in the media. I know that was the result of prayer. I was completely broken. From occasions as small as choosing clothes to decisions as large as choosing a lawyer to handle the numerous legal issues confronting me–God answered my every prayer. Conversation with God blossomed from a daily activity to a constant activity.

I have also experienced God in the gift of friends who have gently, but firmly held me accountable in my relationship with God. Friends have studied Scripture with me, prayed with me, prayed for me, and alerted me in moments that revealed my attitude turning toward self-pity instead of God and the grace and provision with which I am blessed.

As I have traveled this dark and rocky valley, I am keenly aware that God has carried me through. I am so thankful that I am provided, by grace, a dynamic relationship with God that allows me to rest in His loving arms, knowing His provisions will be all I need and knowing they will be best for me, as God carries me through.

John 15:5 "I am the vine; you are the branches. If a man remains in me and I in him, he will bear much fruit." NIV

The Results Of Free Will

Nothing in Scripture is as confounding to me as free will. Why would God create us this way? God clearly has the will for all of us to be in relationship with Him. From the Garden of Eden, through the giving of the law, to Calvary, God continually demonstrates this desire to be in relationship with us and His willingness to make the way clear. Nevertheless, to make the relationship truly a relationship, we must enter into it by our choice. Therefore, we are created with the free will to choose to either follow or not follow God.

Just as a tiny pebble ripples a whole pond–all choices affect many more than those we consider. When my husband was killed, I lost my husband, my children lost their dad, my sister lost her deeply loved brother-in-law, my in-laws lost their son, his sisters lost their brother, my parents lost a son-in-law, high school students lost their Sunday school teacher, professionals lost a coworker, and the ripples continued beyond our view. Free will to choose the relationship with God also means we live in a fallen and imperfect world. Because of the misuse of freewill and our resulting state of existence, tragedy and struggles happen. Our world is no longer the perfect Garden of Eden. Therefore, disease plagues us, disaster strikes, accidents happen to our loved ones, and the imperfection of our world strikes each of us. This is not God's doing; it is a result of living

in a fallen world, the product of free will and human choice. We
are not subject to divine punishment, but rather human choice
and evil. At some point in every life, we each encounter tragedy
of some degree.

My first brush with tragedy came in my early adulthood.
I was in my first teaching job in the inner city area of Southern
California. A lovely thirteen-year-old girl who had been in my
choir class for three years was doing all she could to stay the
course of success. She was accomplished in school and stayed
out of the gang life. Yet because of gang retaliation against her
father, who lived in another area, she was shot and killed in a
drive-by shooting. The fact that we often do not create our own
tragedy became a stark reality. Tragedy hits, and it is not selec-
tive. We cannot indulge in the fantasy that faith gives us a "get
out of tragedy free" card. Nothing about Christ's teachings or
example would support that thinking.

In fact, Christ's teachings prepare us for difficulty, and His
crucifixion demonstrates that even the most pure and holy suffer. Further, we must accept that living in a fallen world, with
free will, means that we live with people who use their free will
to turn away from God. All good comes from God, but not all
actions come from God. Humans exercise free will to turn from
God, even to generate truly evil acts. There is no logic or solid
theology in attributing acts of evil to the hand of God–particularly in a fallen world established by the human exercise of
free will. God provides many promises in Scripture, but an easy,
struggle-free road is not one of them. Fortunately for us, some of
the promises made include a Comforter to guide us and strength
to endure the inevitable difficulties. Scripture tells us God knows
there will be suffering.

I have lived tragedy, and I can tell you that I have not faced it alone or by having to rely on my own wisdom or strength to endure. This is where we see God's will. God's will is for us to be in relationship with Him, thereby, never alone in times of tragedy. Our connection to God, reliance upon God, and relationship with God becomes what defines us, not the tragedy we endure.

I know what it is to be broken by tragedy. In the week that Elan's body was missing and I was seeking a missing person, I was as broken as a human could have been. I felt like my whole life was falling apart. One morning I told my mother I was going upstairs to take my shower and to get ready to go out searching again. As I started into the bathroom, I froze at the door. The bathroom was empty. Every morning for fourteen years, Elan would shave while I took my shower. The bathroom was empty. Elan had always been there, and the bathroom was empty. I collapsed on the floor into a curled up heap and sobbed. I just could not face that empty bathroom. My mother waited, and after a long while of not hearing the shower water running, she came in to check on me and found me on the floor sobbing. I was so broken I could not even bathe myself. Through my mother, at that moment, God picked me up and got me through that day. And in the days, weeks, and now years since, God has used many of His faithful witnesses to put me back on my feet and on a road He directs me to travel. Faith in God does not promise a smooth, easy road. In fact, the role of freewill and the value of our choosing God daily become clearer to us as we grow in relationship to God and travel the road fraught with tragedy that each of us must face. As we make the decision to choose God daily, we grow in our ability to see God's hand providing, guiding, and sustaining. We also find a growth and maturity as we pass through the dark valleys with God.

A track hoe driver not taking all the precautions he should have buried my husband under large pieces of cement that should have been carried off the work site along with tons of dirt. That was not God's will. That was the will of men trying to hurry and trying to cut corners. That was not God's will. Human will, human greed, human error, human selfishness is what caused those slabs of cement and dirt to bury my husband. It was definitely not God's will. The logical question then is this: What is God's will? The moment the cement hit, God's will for Elan to spend eternity with Him was realized. Neither height nor depth can separate us from the love of God. As Elan's body was buried, God was there taking Elan into eternal joy. That was God's will. Friends who cared for my family, in my home, and putting family up in their own homes–that was God's will. Police officers who would not give up until we knew exactly what happened–that was God's will. Friends who sat with me at the construction site, prayed with me as the media asked questions, and sat with me in my home at night were all a part of God's will. The man who rose early every morning to fix sausage rolls and eggs for my family and friends and delivered them hot to my house before anyone could begin to worry about what to fix for breakfast, the pastor from a nearby church who brought lunch to the work site, the lady at the local grocery store who sent coffee and hot chocolate, the friend who brought in an additional track hoe and a driver to aid in the search, these were God's will. The church that continued to provide meals for months, the men from my church that take care of my pool, the lady from my church who cooks my meals now, the youth from my church who mows my yard, the youth who provide babysitting, the friends who help take care of my children when I get sick, the lady who came to watch my children–and brought donuts–so I could get yard work done—these are examples of God's will. I would not be honest if I allowed anything other than the truth. All I have shared here is only a fraction of the numerous ways God's will of provision and sustenance demonstrates itself continually.

God's will has included friendships with precious people who have lost husbands and are a wonderful resource for me. Other precious people who lost their dads as young children also provide wisdom and guidance for me. God's will is that I will never be alone. God's will is to sustain, provide, guide, and comfort my children and me. God's will is being realized in our lives. We have had and continue to have peace, peace that passes understanding, and that is from God alone.

Free will still confounds me, but I do know that human will and God's will are not one in the same. Knowing this, we must be intentional with regard to our exercise of our own will. We must clearly choose the relationship with God every day. We must make that relationship a priority over the exercise of human choice.

I know that human will and living in an imperfect fallen world generates tragedy. I am certain that God's will for each of us is to sustain, comfort, provide, and guide us through tragedy. It involves helping us grow and mature during these difficult times. God's will involves abundant joy for you, endurance for the hard times, becoming what God had in mind when He created you in spite of tragedy, and even maturing your faith so that you can glorify Him and have an impact on the bigger picture of the eternal kingdom. That is God's will for us all.

John 16:33–"In this world you will have trouble. But take heart! I have overcome the world." NIV

The Pain And The Sound Of Peace

As I walked down the aisle at the funeral home, I was wracked with painful flashbacks. Only months earlier I had stood exactly where she was standing, greeting many of the same people who surrounded us now, at the visitation for my husband's funeral. Now I approached my friend, knowing there were no words of wisdom, no verbal gift I could give. She had lost her beautiful daughter in a senseless boating accident. There was nothing to say. I reached her, and reached for her. As I hugged her, she spoke softly words I could deeply understand. "When I first saw the boat, I felt God reach down and hold me in His hands, and He hasn't let me go."

"I know," I responded.

She looked into my eyes with her tear-filled eyes, "I knew you would understand."

I understood. I remembered that sense of being carried, transported as if by a divine escalator, from moment-to-moment, day-to-day. Tragedy struck, evil played its hand, and then in a twisted irony, the clock kept ticking. Time continued, and life still had to be lived, but how would we do that? The tragedy was so overwhelming that nothing seemed the same. Nothing is the same. We are not walking on our own. We are carried by God. Despite the intense pain, we experienced peace, a peace that defies all reason or logic. This peace, God's divine peace, becomes a guiding force for our new way of living.

Through the weeks, months, and now years after my husband's death, I have lacked absolutely nothing. Every need of mine and of my children has been met. Not so that we bypassed the pain and the tragedy, but rather, we tangibly experienced the reality that we were not passing through this valley alone.

The apostle Paul began each of his letters with "Grace and peace to you." The words "peace to you" came from a man who lost wealth and who was beaten, imprisoned, and persecuted. Paul went from the upper crust to the bottom of the societal order. Yet Paul writes about peace and initiates all correspondence with a prayer for grace and peace. Paul writes in Philippians (chapter 4) about a contentment that does not rely on circumstance. That contentment is a divine centering—a placing of one's entire self into God's hands and care. As Paul writes, we can find strength to do anything through the strength given to us by God. It takes courage and the strength of God to face the intense pain of tragedy and walk through it. God gives us that courage and strength, and then God gives us more. He gives us divine peace.

As the tragedy of my husband's death threw my world into a chaotic whirlwind, I was wrapped in an overwhelming sense of peace—not an irrational sense of denial. I had no delusion that suddenly I would awaken from this nightmare, and it would all be over. Neither did I have an unfounded fantasy that the inevitable struggles and heartaches that lie in the years ahead would disappear like a mirage before I reached them. I clearly remember saying to my mother the day they found Elan's body, "I can't do my life without him." I was right. I lost more than my husband, I lost my best friend, my children's security, my spiritual leader and partner, many other friends, my music ministry position, and every birthday I'll encounter in the future. In addition, the losses continue as milestones of life are reached for my children, and their dad is not there to celebrate with them. As all three of us reach points in our lives where his presence would make such a tremendous difference, we suffer loss again and again. Despite all those losses, I never lost peace. That peace that transcends human reason enveloped me, secured me, and continues to do so today.

Prior to Elan's death, my relationship with God, my theology, held that God could and would provide for every need I encountered. The provision may not be exactly what I want, but it will be exactly what is best for me. All I have lived in this tragedy has proved this correct. At the hand of God, I have experienced provision for every true need. Amazingly, many of the provisions have been for needs I did not realize I had. The need and provision would reveal themselves at the same time.

I recall the first Easter, only months into this journey. A faculty member at the school came to me the week of Easter and asked if I already took care of Easter baskets for my children. I had completely forgotten. I was totally unprepared. She told me she had been praying for a way to help us, and God had put this on her heart. The next day she arrived at school with two wonderfully filled Easter baskets, ready for Easter morning for my children. She continued taking care of Easter baskets the next year too. I had forgotten and didn't even realize I needed help until help was already present. This is just one of the many continual blessings we experienced as God provided all our needs, big and small.

I came to understand through experience that I will go nowhere in the days ahead where Jesus has not already been and made provision for me. This is where the sense of peace has become so crucial. I have come to understand divine peace as a strong, guiding force in living life.

In the dark hours, so many decisions had to be made about important matters—from funeral arrangements to financial planning. My experience was that God would put the person or people in place to make or guide those decisions. God put the thoughts clearly in my head without me having to struggle to be clear on my own. I knew they were God-sent by the overwhelming peace that accompanied them. One such decision was in regards to where I should have Elan's body buried. Common advice led to a large, local cemetery. That cemetery was right across the street from the pre-school my daughter attended. Every day her daddy drove her to school. I knew my infant son would go to that preschool some day. In the midst of the darkness, I clearly knew that my children could not have their father buried there. Further, I had a clear idea of where I should seek a burial sight. Now years later, many ask in amazement, "How did you think of all that?" I know that I didn't. It was a God-guided and peace-supported decision. One of many I had to make as I rested in God's hands through the dark days. When we are at our lowest, Scripture tells us that the Holy Spirit will intercede. We will be comforted and prayers will be lifted on our behalf. We will experience the peace that passes understanding.

> *Romans 8:26 "In the same way the spirit helps us in our weakness. We do not know what we ought to pray for, but the Spirit himself intercedes for us with groans that words cannot express." NIV*

When we are not in the dark, we live with the illusion that we can reason and think on our own just fine. The truth is, whether in dark hours or bright times, our human reasoning and thinking is just human, and therefore flawed. We need to be reliant on the guidance of God in the whisperings and urgings of the Holy Spirit. We need to confirm our decisions, urged by the Holy Spirit, by the test of peace. Divine, guiding peace is much like learning to drive with a teacher in the car with you. While ultimately we are the ones driving the road of our lives, we are well served to follow the directions and advice of the instructor. When we follow the leading of peace, we navigate the road of life much better. In the darkest moments of our lives, when we know we are broken to the point we have no business driving at all, that is the time we can best experience total dependence on God's guidance and peace. As the darkness turns to dawn, this dependence is something we need to nurture and on which we need to focus. We must purposefully seek to find peace in our decisions rather than human reason.

The peace God gives does not give us a shortcut to the dawn. The darkness of night is still the length of a night. The peace of God does not provide a shield from pain. The hurt of tragedy that pulls us into the dark hours is just as intense. However, the peace does provide comfort as we rest in God's hands as we are transported through the dark. Further, the peace provides decisiveness when we seek to remain within God's direction as we navigate the darkness. I was at peace with the many decisions I had to make, and they have all proven beneficial for me. Some decisions were easy, like to seek and use the advice of a financial planner to help me become stable on my teacher's income. Others were more painful, such as resigning my position as the music minister at my church after eight years there. That decision was particularly painful, yet I was completely at peace with it. After I resigned, the benefit to my children and me became clear. I could not have seen it or reasoned this ahead of receiving the benefit; I simply followed what I knew brought peace.

One hard aspect of living by the divine guidance of peace is the lack of worldly understanding. While I would feel led by God to make specific choices and have that reinforced by overwhelming peace, many would still question. They would want reason or logic to explain my decisions. I would, and still can, only offer that those decisions provided peace. It is challenging to act on what you believe God is leading you to do, based on the logic and reason of the peace that passes all understanding. Directions of a driving instructor don't always seem understandable, yet as a student, we comply. We need to seek God in the same manner. In your darkest hours, turn to Him, listen for His guidance in the gentle whisper, and feel His affirmation in the peace that passes all understanding. When the world questions, hold on to that which brings peace.

Cast yourself upon Him and let Him carry you through the darkest hours, days, months, and years. More than that, continue to seek the peace that comes when you invite God to teach you, guide you, and navigate life's road for you.

John 14:27 "Peace I leave you; my peace I give you. I do not give to you as the world gives. Do not let your hearts be troubled and do not be afraid." NIV

Growing In The Dark

The practice was the same almost every night. I would pick up and clean up around the downstairs of the house, stacking everything that belonged upstairs at the bottom of the stairs. Then in one totally ridiculous attempt, I would try to carry it all upstairs, by myself, as Elan watched. He would chuckle as I loaded a gym bag, a few books, a stack of folded laundry, some mail, a half-a-dozen toys, a pair of shoes and dirty socks, and a freshly poured glass of ice water into my hands. Then I would start up the stairs. Amongst the spilling water, falling toys, and his chuckles, I would hear, "I could get some of that." My nightly response was as equally predictable as his chuckles. "No, I can do this."

"I can do this" was my motto. Nothing stood in my way. I could work my way through college. I could get the impossible master's degree. I could—and then I found myself in a broken heap, sobbing because I could not face my empty bedroom. Tragedy transforms everything and everyone. I now know how absurd those nightly journeys up the stairs were. I now see why it would have been so much better not to do it all myself. I learned this in the darkest moments of my life. When tragedy strikes, our first decision is either to cry out to God or to blame God. A sound theology, recognizing that free will generated the fallen state of our existence, leaves only one response. Reach to

God and allow Him to sustain you. While God provides for us and sustains us in the dark times, God also can heal us. As we travel the dark valley in God's care, we are not simply transported from entry to exit. God can heal our wounded hearts and transform our weeping into shouts of joy.

Nothing illuminates our need for healing like the darkness of tragedy. In the darkness, we are keenly aware of the brokenness and pain stemming from the tragedy that plunged us into the dark. God attends that pain and comforts us. God comforted me with the presence of the Holy Spirit and the presence of family members who stayed with me so I would not have to spend a night alone until I was ready. He comforted me with church family and friends who consistently provided comfort when I needed it. God also attended to my brokenness—first with His own healing touch that allowed me to miraculously pick up and move one step at a time in a forward motion. Next God used a few calls to speak publicly and offer myself in ministry as moments of affirmation that God could still have purpose and direction for me in the future. God also provided healing of the obvious brokenness by connecting me with a Christian grief counselor for my children and me. God took charge of the obvious pain and brokenness that needed attention and healing.

The darkness did another strange thing. It illuminated other areas that needed healing as well. We cannot experience healing until we know we are sick. For many, the illness we live with from day-to-day is hidden in worldly ideals that are applauded. Hidden illnesses get covered by our "I can do it" mottos. We do not even realize that we need healing for the illness of self-sufficiency or self-reliance. Regardless of the applause of the world, we do. When we become secure in our self and our ability to accomplish, instead of secure in God and God's ability to accomplish, we are in need of healing. When we live in the delusion that we can plan, organize, schedule, and be in control of our lives and the lives of those we love, we are in need of healing, and we don't even know it. What is worse, we are admired for the very thing that causes us to need healing. It is a difficult illness to spot.

The darkness put a spotlight on my illness of self-reliance and being in control. For the first time in my adult life, I was only able to say, "Could you please do that?" and "I can't do that." I know in the days immediately after my husband was killed, I was, for the first time in my life, wholly and completely dependant on God.   From February 22 to the first part of June, I did not even choose what to eat or wear for myself. Matthew 6:25–34 tells us we do not need to concern ourselves with those needs. I realize now that I always took that metaphorically, not literally. Now in the darkness, I was living it literally. I learned to not do it all myself. I don't continually say, "I can do it." In fact, I gladly look around now to find those near me who God has equipped with graces, gifts, and talents, and I ask for their help. Not only does this give others the opportunity to minister and bless people with their God-given talents, it reminds me that I need to give God the credit. We all need to accept the fact that every time we take the "I can do it" approach, we also take the "I did that" credit. If we are to be God powered and God driven, then there is no room for the "I did that" moments of self-reliance.

This healing has been a God-sized accomplishment. In fact, many who knew me prior to Elan's death deem this change in me as an absolute miracle. Somewhere in the darkness, I put down my need to be in control of everything, and I stopped saying, "I can do it." God healed an illness I did not even know I had. The remarkable part of it all is that I experience much more peace and genuine divine joy. When I hear and follow God, the peace is deep and wonderful. When I am blessed by His hand with provisions I would not have even known to ask for, the abundant joy is unspeakable. It is in the desperate darkness that we can best learn the authentic nature of the divine joy that God provides. In the darkness, we learn how much more valuable, divine joy is than any other experience or possession this world offers.

The darkness also put a spotlight on another illness that required God's healing hand, the illness of chaos. Our society breeds chaos—overbooked schedules, weeks packed with activities, lessons, practices, and meetings. We make scheduled times for our children to play. We rush, divide, and conquer—carpool, fast food, and action—all crammed into our days. Society is producing stressed out children and unhealthy adults. I was right in the middle of it all, doing as much as the rest of you. Over-scheduled, under-rested, and doing it all. At one point, I was teaching at a full-time job, working a part-time church job, raising a daughter, attending graduate school, playing in two soccer leagues, and coaching a girls' soccer team as well. I was doing it all.

God is calling to us and offering peace. God offers order. We scramble and generate chaos and call it overachieving. Genesis introduces us to a God of order. God separates and places boundaries and divisions. God orders all things. God offers peace. God tells us to take a day of rest, but we have too much to do to take a day of rest. We wear our illness of chaos like a badge of honor, until we face tragedy and realize that in the chaos we lose precious moments that we can never have back. The morning my husband left for work for the last time was a busy morn-

72

ing. Chaos had won. As we all rushed for the door, I was too busy and too late to stop and kiss him good-by. It was one of only a handful of times in our married life I had allowed us to part that way, but I was busy. Chaos robbed me of my last kiss. God has healed much of that hurt, but most importantly, God has healed me of chaos. I hold my children; I sit down on the couch. I still spend most evenings straightening up the house, but I spend more time sitting with my children reading a book, playing a game, or praying. I also bought myself a big basket that I use to put things in to carry them up the stairs.

We generate for ourselves a busy, attractive life of chaos. When things get bad we, as humans, usually try to fix it ourselves with self-sufficiency and by taking control. If that doesn't stop the hurt from coming in, we just keep moving and get real busy. When things get tragic, we must cry out to God and allow God to provide all we need and to heal us of our affliction. God reaches us in the darkness, allows the darkness to illuminate our needs, and then God heals us. We may still be in the darkness tragedy produces; that darkness does not change–but we do. God heals us, we gain hope, and we are changed. Moreover, when the darkness gives way to dawn, we emerge transformed.

Psalm 59:16–17–"But I will sing of thy might; I will sing aloud of thy steadfast love in the morning. For thou hast been to me a fortress and a refuge in the day of my distress. O my Strength, I will sing praises to thee, for thou, O God, art my fortress, the God who shows me steadfast love." RSV

Reconstruction

In my Bible, there is a special marker, a purple ribbon with a silver charm on the end that reads, "Lord, teach me to pray." The marker is special, but the place it marks is even more meaningful. It marks James 1:2–4. *"My brothers and sisters whenever you face trials of any kind, consider it nothing but joy, because you know that the testing of your faith produces endurance; and let endurance have it's full effect, so that you may be mature and complete, lacking in nothing." (NRSV)*

In the dark valley, when we listen for God in the still, small voice and allow peace to be a guiding force, much can happen. In the dark, we experience total dependence on God, and that can be transforming. In that dependence, we experience growth and maturing we never imagined, and that is where God can work on our reconstruction and restoration.

Through these times, we learn to release our need to be in control, we learn to gain strength from the wind, and we learn to allow God to heal us and move us forward in the direction He would choose. I have honestly experienced a peculiar sense of joy in this dark valley, because I can feel the hand of God not just healing me, but shaping a growth and establishing a reconstruction that is exciting and beyond any growth of faith I had ever imagined.

James 1:2–4 tells us that the trials produce endurance. They do. If you have already faced tragedy, you know exactly what I mean. I would wake up many days and feel more tired than when I tried to go to sleep. My first thought was that I could not possibly make it even one more day. Then the end of that day arrived, and I faced the next day. Endurance begins to develop. Tragedy and trials produce the same growth in our faith. Our faith becomes stronger and capable of much greater endurance. You don't know how to cast all your cares upon God until you are in a place where the only way to get up each day is to do just that—completely rely on God to carry the load. Trials produce a strengthening of our faith. God does not generate trials; our fallen world does that. Do not mistake this, though, God will use the trials in our lives for our good. Sometimes "our good," what is truly best for us, is a longer struggle than we want. God wants us to grow, and to grow in relationship with Him. Therefore, He loves us enough to allow us to go through the pain, not allowing us to bypass the pain. This is for our own good. Think of the self-control God must have to let human free will run its course and cause its pain. In that pain, when we choose to call upon God, God steps in to nurture us and guide us as we mature in faith. We learn to fully rely on God and follow God's leadings instead of our human impulses, and then God's will is realized as we run to Him freely. God weeps with us in our pain and sorrow and waits for our willingness to follow Him as He leads us to growth in the darkness and his reconstruction of our lives.

I don't believe I am alone in my struggle with wanting to be in control, although I probably struggle more than most. I'll confess; it is even very hard for me to ride in a car with someone.

I do better when I drive. I have been accused of being compulsive in my need to be in control, and many of those accusations are more accurate than I want to admit. However, my time in the darkness has produced growth in this area. Completely broken, I could no longer hide behind the façade of "I have this under control" or "I can do this." I had to face a truth that had been true all along—only God has it under control. The quickest way for me to make a mess of a situation is for me to do it all myself. When we try to do it all or we try to have things under control, we are really seeking to gain a sense of freedom. When Elan was killed, I broke. I could no longer pretend to be in control. In fact, all I could do was rely completely on God. God provided, and I was absolved of the weight of maintaining the façade of control. Freedom and joy came to me through placing my broken self in God's hands and letting Him be in control. The pain and brokenness brought me to that place as nothing else could. Learning to allow God to be in control was a major part of God's reconstruction for me.

Darkness produced a growth that I could never have imagined. Just as free will is to benefit our relationship with God by allowing us to choose the relationship, this relinquishing of our desire to be in control also has relational benefit. When we allow God to be in control, we move into a deeper relationship with God, which pleases God because He wants us closer. We gain the joy of God's pleasure and the peace of moving closer to God. We trust God to do both the navigating and the driving, and the ride becomes much more pleasurable.

In the darkness, we most accurately grasp the vastness of our need, and that produces a new level of thankfulness. It is the broken who are thankful for restoration, the weeping who are thankful for joy, and neither needs to be in control of the restoration or joy. In the darkness of tragedy, we come face-to-face with our real human condition. We are not in control, and we are powerless to stop the pain. Only in God's hands can we experience genuine healing, and by God's grace and provision, we experience restoration and joy. In the darkness, we can grow to a maturity that allows us to put God in control of our lives as restoration takes place.

With God in control of our lives, we put ourselves in His hands for a healing that produces strength and maturity. We will gain strength from God's healing. Weight lifting for athletic training and strengthening is an interesting science. What weight lifting accomplishes in the actual workout is a series of tears in the muscles. The gain occurs when healing takes place. As the muscles heal, they are made stronger than before the workout. God can accomplish the same with our faith. As the healing occurs, our faith is stronger than before the damaging tragedy.

The scientific project of the biosphere yielded some information that applies here as well. It seems that an absence of wind caused the trees to grow weak and the stems of the fruit to be so weak that the fruit fell off the trees before it had a chance to ripen. There was no wind to generate a need for strength in the trunks or the fruit stems. We are like those trees. Without wind, we grow weak and the fruit we could bear doesn't ripen to its full potential. In the dark and facing the wind, the last thing on our minds is thankfulness for the strength we are gaining. While facing the wind, we should try to focus on thanking God for the strength He can give us in these times. Thankfulness is another element of God's restoration in my life. I have come to a place of thankfulness that I had never known before.

The greatest gusts of wind I have faced and still face are the strong winds of loneliness. The loneliness has been absolutely horrible at times. I have been rejected and abandoned by most of my old friends, and I feel almost like a leper–alone and hopeless because there is no societal place for me. I don't fit in anywhere. Although welcomed, I'm too young for the widows club. I can't get every other weekend and one night a week free to fit in with divorced parents, and I don't deal with many of the struggles and issues they do. I am not a single; I'm a family, but I don't fit in with the married two-parent families. Just like the leper, I only have the hope of the healing touch of Jesus. That is where the healing and growing God provides is most powerful, when we know our hope is in Jesus' touch.

In the darkness, I have experienced a new level of emotional dependence on God. When the gusts of loneliness blow, and they blow often, there is only one place to turn, to the touch of Christ. Like many, my initial reaction to the pain of loneliness was to run from it. Getting busy and keeping lots of people around me became my approach. As God healed me and led me to grow during this time, I have become at peace with being still. God gives me the strength and comfort to face the gusts of loneliness. I have learned by God's hand to accept the lonely days and cry out to Him during those times. While I have managed to see much of my world improve in the areas of running my household and parenting my children more effectively, I am still without a partner. God looked at Adam, saw that he was alone, and decided that was not good. God is right. The loneliness is probably the hardest aspect I have had to cope with. The pain of it is intense. Yet God reaches out and touches my aching heart with His comfort, and the darkness proves itself as a place to grow again as I learn to rely on God for the deepest emotional need I have. God is with me, and I am not alone. Each time I reach out for the healing touch of Jesus in the lonely moments, God accomplishes further restoration and reconstruction.

While in the darkness, I have also grown in the area of following God. Reconstruction in my heart and life has been tough and has required a lot of prayerful self-examination. I had to face bits of myself that I had learned to ignore, and now I must confront them. Some areas I didn't even realize were so much a part of me—like my self-consciousness and discomfort with my physical appearance. God has and continues to work with me on addressing and dealing with these areas. Just like the journey through the darkness, this is a long process. After I confront one habit or way of thinking, God shows me another. I am continually moving through these areas, giving them over to God. This process repeats itself, because I can only give over to God the things of which I am aware. As I do that, God moves me forward and into another area. The movement from one area to another is one of God's most amazing reconstruction accomplishments. In the process of healing, I have moved forward, closer to a faith that is complete, mature, and lacking in nothing. I have also moved forward literally. God has led me through decisions about work, schedules, and habits. Forward progress is made in reducing the time commitments I used to keep, while spending more time with family and most importantly with God.

I find myself in awe at the work of God's hand in the reconstruction of my heart. God has truly taken the shattered pieces of my heart and reconstructed a new work. It is still a work in progress, but the fingerprints of God are all over what has been accomplished thus far. I enjoy trusting God and not being in control. I am thankful for God's ability to carry my load. I have learned to be thankful for the wind as it makes me stronger. I marvel at the way God can reveal to me areas in which I can grow and mature, hopefully becoming more like what He had in mind when He created me. I am continually amazed at the way God can heal my lonely heart when I place my hope in Him. The reconstruction is a long process, one I am thankful for, and not willing to rush.

> *Php.3:12 "Not that I have already obtained this or have already reached the goal; but I press on to make it my own, because Christ Jesus has made me his own." NRSV*

Hearing God and Following

I have always marveled, since the first time I heard the story during my childhood, at the account of the calling of the first disciples. Jesus said, "Follow me," and they immediately dropped their nets and followed. I don't know about you, but to me that seems bizarre. I know of the scholarly discussions surrounding this story—rationalizations for the disciples' responses. However, none of the explanations seem to approach the amazing and simple statement "Immediately they dropped their nets and followed Him." The statement is simple, yet astounding.

From the instant I realized that my husband was late getting home to the moment I am writing this, there is a long path of steps I have walked only because God said, "Follow me here." In an earlier chapter, I discussed hearing God's voice, telling me, "He is not here" as I started looking for Elan. When I chose to ignore that and went my own direction, God did not give up on me. God continued to shelter me and provide for me. I could not find peace until I listened to God's voice and followed. Eventually, I resigned myself to listening because God had already spoken to my heart. I believe that no matter how hard I tried to run from it, I knew.

When I listened, I knew that my task was to help the police recover his body. I went to the construction site on Thursday afternoon with a completely different approach. I was finally listening and following. For the first time, instead of looking for a missing person, I studied the photographs of the trenches taken from Elan's field camera. I walked the area with Elan's coworker and carefully examined the photos. I listened for the nudges of the Holy Spirit. I saw the trenches and the photos with a new clarity. It was at that time that I felt strongly led to question one particular area of the recovery digging. I remember it clearly today. It was as if God turned on a light for me, and I saw that one trench had not been re-opened correctly. First, I had a long discussion with Elan's coworker, explaining what I saw. Convinced of what I was seeing, I called a police officer over and told him where I felt they needed to dig. It was late in the afternoon. The police officer told me they would start there the next morning. By 9:15 the next morning, his body was recovered.

God had shown me where to go, and I am so thankful I followed. I could have lived the rest of my life wondering where Elan was; now by God's leading and grace, I could have peace. That was only the beginning. God led me to a conversation with a friend who guided my response to the legal aspects resulting from not having a will and a wrongful death investigation. God led my children and me to an amazing grief counselor. She helped us work through so many difficult issues and helped us gain so many valuable tools to face our future. I am so thankful I followed God when He said, "Follow me to counseling."

Not all of the following has been easy, and I have not always been quick to respond. God has not withdrawn His request to "Follow me" at any point. At times, I just chose the nets instead. God gave me numerous opportunities to lessen the load of maintaining my home. In my stubbornness and desire to be in control, I clung to the nets. I hung on to those nets until I could no longer carry them. One by one, I put down the nets. I found easier ways to get meals prepared. I followed God's leading into getting help with yard care, house cleaning, and even childcare. God kept saying for me to follow, and the more I did, the more at peace both my children and I became.

Then there were God's calls to follow that were heart wrenching. Letting go of old friendships that were proving unhealthy was the first call. Confronting the loneliness instead of running from it and keeping busy was the next. The biggest "Follow me" was in my ministry appointment. For eight years, I had served a church in music ministry. Those years encompassed the growth of my daughter from infancy to second grade and the birth of my son. I was emotionally tied to the church, as well as my position as music minister. This time of music ministry overlapped the time spent in seminary and ministry candidacy. As I struggled to heal and care for my children, I heard God telling my heart that I needed to put it down. That was the longest wrestling match with the nets I could identify since my husband's death. Since Elan's death, I had not had the strength or desire to wrestle with God for long periods until this one. God would provide, sustain, and lead, and I followed. I didn't follow out of amazing discipleship; I followed as a living example of how, in our weakness, He is strong. Now God was leading me down a scary and difficult road. I hung on to those nets. I wrestled with those nets. Finally, after nearly a year, I put them down and followed. I am still uncertain what my ministry will involve. I am certain that I will do my best to listen to His leading and to follow.

Hebrews 12:1 " . . . let us run with perseverance the race marked out for us."NIV

God knows the race that is set before us. I am sure that I

am better off not knowing how long that race is or how many hurdles are involved in it. God will sustain me the length of the race and provide what I need to get over the hurdles. If I had seen this stretch of the race that is just ahead of me, I certainly would have failed even to start running. Not only does God know the race ahead, God knows how to use the trials and pain to transform and strengthen each of us and make us more complete in our faith. I finally put the nets down and followed God in the call regarding my ministry appointment. I do not have a new position, and I don't know when or if I will again in the future. What I do know is that God is guiding my steps, and He will lead me in the race He has for me. Meanwhile, I am growing in my trust and strengthening in my ability to rest completely in His guidance and provision.

I have discovered that the more I follow, the more I become equipped to follow. Those who encounter God, God's leading, and the joy of being where God intends for them to be, are changed. They desire to stay in the path God leads and the peace and joy that path provides. When you follow God, your heart is changed. God infuses you with strength where you previously knew weakness. God enables you to forgive where you knew you only felt anger and bitterness. God teaches you to become skilled at submission instead of proficient at self-directedness and being in control. Most importantly, God educates us in the value of his abundant joy and teaches us to treasure that joy over worldly gain and applause.

In the time since I resigned from my ministry appointment, I have baked cookies with my children, listened to my daughter talk to me about anything and everything, and taught my son to love praying. Mostly, I have grown in my ability to slow down and trust God, to be still and know that God is God, to know that deep in my heart. God could not heal my heart until I stopped and found time to worship Him and to be fed.

God knows the plans He has for you. As bizarre as it sounds, drop the nets and follow.

Heb. 12:1–2 *"Therefore, since we are surrounded by such a great cloud of witnesses, let us throw off everything that hinders and the sin that so easily entangles, and let us run with perseverance the race marked out for us. Let us fix our eyes on Jesus, the author and perfector of our faith"* NIV

Time for Sanctuary

It's a noisy world. Phones ring at home, at work, in your purse, or on your belt. Music blasts, advertisers compete for our attention, and our computers are joining in. That is only the tip of our noise iceberg. We long for a moment like the scenes on vacation advertising, solitude with someone who adores us on a secluded beach or a mountain retreat. Not to give the travel advertisers too much credit, but that is exactly what we need, solitude with the One who loves us best so we can listen.

I Kings, Chapter 19, gives us a story that applies to our lives. Elijah, the prophet, has run. He is fleeing from Jezebel who has threatened to kill him. I know that most of us are not fleeing a death threat. Although, many of us have stress levels that we know threaten our health and our lives. We run. Life can get crazy. Elijah shows us the value of sanctuary. He goes out alone to Mount Horeb and spends the night in a cave. God speaks to him, telling him to go out and stand on the mountain in the presence of the Lord, because the Lord is about to pass by. Then came the huge winds, but God was not in the wind. The winds blow around us too. An earthquake is Elijah's next experience, but God is not in the earthquake. We certainly get our share of earthquakes. Then came a fire, and God was not in the fire. Many of us know the fire today as well. Then came the gentle whisper. Some translations of Scripture read "the sound of sheer silence." The important point is that the sound is not loud. Compared to the sounds of the world, the sound is incredibly soft. Then Elijah received instruction and direction from the Lord, as well as assurance and confidence. When we get apart from the confusion and past the noise, wind, earthquakes, and fires of living, we can place ourselves in a position to listen. It is a place that enables us to commune with God, listen for the gentle whisper, and find sanctuary.

Sanctuary is that place where you are able to be still and know that God is God. Sanctuary is that place where you can hear God in the sheer silence. Sanctuary is the place where, when you leave, you know you have been in God's presence. That kind of sanctuary takes an effort to discover and is more valuable than words could ever describe.

My earliest experience with sanctuary came during my final year of teaching in southern California. After the death of one of my students, emotional pain became an intense struggle. When I felt the waves of emotional pain swell, I would go to the ocean and sit alone, listening to the waves and God's comfort and direction. Once I moved to teach in Texas, I discovered sanctuary in the mountains of my childhood state. Annual trips to spend time in the mountains became a priority. When the tragedy of my husband's death hit, intense struggles followed. Sanctuary in the mountains became vital and more frequent. I found myself having to deal with decisions related to the wrongful death lawsuit that overwhelmed me. I knew that worldly advice and direction could not be my guide. I had to hear God. I had to find sanctuary. I went to great lengths to get to the sanctuary of the mountains at key times.

Everyone needs sanctuary. In tragic times, we recognize this need more readily. The value of sanctuary is the same regardless of the situation, and we should make sanctuary a vitally important part of our lives. Sanctuary is the place where we hear God because the noise of the world is shut out. God still speaks in the gentle whisper, so we need to discover two forms of sanctuary and make them priorities. One is daily sanctuary, where we can focus on God's leading and listen for the gentle whispers. The second is isolated sanctuary in a sacred place that can be enjoyed for several days in a block. These are the times where God can convict us, direct us, and energize us. The benefit of sanctuary is a heart that can hear the whispers that often don't even fall into words, just a heartfelt knowing.

Daily sanctuary requires two efforts. You must discover what works for you, and then you must protect that time in your daily routine. What works for one may not work for another. You must seek out the time and place that produces the most quiet and clarity for you. Some people discover that morning is best. Others need midday and others night. Some people need coffee and stillness; others need to exercise. Discovering sanctuary takes effort. Sanctuary time cannot replace study and devotional time or prayer time. That is not to say it cannot be in conjunction with those, but it cannot replace them. Once you find the time and place that you can daily seek sanctuary with God, then you must protect that time in your daily routine. If your time is early morning, then you must protect your daily routine and guard against late nights that produce fatigue and temptation to sleep in and miss your appointed quiet time with God.

In my daily time of sanctuary, I came to hear God clearly and easily in thoughts, in heartfelt convictions, in nudges, and in urgings. During the first few days that Elan was missing, and the backhoe driver reported that Elan had been abducted; I truly felt as if I could not hear God. While I was immersed in God's provisions, surrounded by God's support, and blessed by strength and direction from God, I could not hear God the way I had become accustomed to. After five days of what seemed to me to be unbearable silence, I spoke to my mother about it. I told her that I couldn't hear God. She pointed out that I had been skipping my daily sanctuary time. The next morning, I spent time in sanctuary with God before heading into the chaos of the police search. Within minutes, my heart rediscovered what it had been convicted of days before. I knew that Elan had been killed and not abducted.

The clarity of communication that one can gain from daily sanctuary is phenomenal. Through daily sanctuary, one can connect to God in a way that becomes vital to a healthy relationship with God.

Despite daily sanctuary, the noise of the world can crescendo to a volume that requires a block of sanctuary time in a sacred place. Sacred place sanctuary journeys also require discovery and protection. The idea of a sacred place is not original or new. Pilgrimage is found throughout Scripture and faith history. Often, our modern rush and overloaded schedules erase the notion from our lives completely. This is something we really cannot afford. We first must make the effort to discover the location of our sacred place. Where do you feel that you are in the place God made to fit you? I find that place is in the mountains, a particular lake in the mountains of the state where I grew up. I know others who find it in the desert and others who find it at the coast. The ways we experience God vary in these places also. The list of places is as vast as God's created earth. The task is to discover your sacred place. Then you must protect that sacred journey in your establishment of priorities. The journey there becomes a priority that you don't allow to slip. When you go to that sacred place, keep it sacred. Leave work at home, turn off the cell phone, and luxuriate in the sanctuary of God.

This had become an annual priority for my family prior to tragedy. It became more than vital during the early part of dealing with all that our tragedy dealt us. As well as grieving and helping my children grieve and adjusting to living without my best friend, partner, and soul mate, I had legal issues. The wrongful death suit was a dark cloud at times. At the stormiest point in that struggle, I needed to make decisions that were monumental. I prayed and sought daily sanctuary and felt certain I knew what God was leading me to do. Despite that, the noise of the world prevented me from gaining the confidence to stand on what I thought was God's leading. Against all convention and practical worldly planning, I packed my children and myself, took a few days off work, took my daughter out of school, and headed for my sacred place up in the mountains. I needed to connect with God and to know. When we arrived, before setting up the campsite, I walked to the edge of the lake with my children. I heard the unmistakable cry of an eagle and watched as the distant spot became clear. The eagle flew directly toward us, circled above us, and then dove to snatch a fish from the water no more than twenty yards away. It flew off to the far side of the lake and its nest. My heart heard God's message so clearly.

Isaiah 40:31 "And they that wait upon the Lord shall renew their strength, they shall mount up with wings as eagles, they shall run and not be weary, they shall walk and not faint." KJV

That has been my favorite verse since high school, and in

that moment at the side of the lake, I gave all my worries to God who showed me that I would indeed be able to count on Him for my daily bread and that He would provide all I needed.

I will not miss my annual journey to my sacred place. Of course, it is not the only place I can find God and experience sanctuary, but it is a sure place. It is my sacred place, and I will seek sanctuary there. As I gaze on the beauty and the majesty of his creation, it is overwhelming that the Creator of it all knows my name. More overwhelming is that the Creator of it all is only a prayer away–and his voice is only a moment of sanctuary away.

I know that when I have been in sanctuary with God I am changed. Just as Moses appeared changed after his time on the mountain, all of us are changed when we encounter God. While I can't speak specifically about a physical change of appearance, there must be a subtle one. I always get comments on how rejuvenated I look or just how relaxed and happy I look. I think this is a physical manifestation of the spiritual transformation that occurs in a sanctuary journey. You truly can tell people who spend time in the presence of God. Time in God's presence does not alter the problems they face or the battles they fight. However, time with God infuses one with a peace that is bigger than the problems they face, and that peace will not suffer defeat in any battle. That peace radiates from them. It is as unmistakable as the cry of the eagle. Sanctuary is the place where you learn to be still and know God.

While this seems most important in times of challenge, don't over look how important it is in the dry, actionless, directionless times of life. These times are unique challenges in and of themselves. The holding pattern phases of life can be depressing and frustrating. I would meet these times with a longer list of things to do. Instead of holding and seeking sanctuary to listen, I would launch into action to make something happen. That reaction is easier than waiting, and it is harmful. Holding pattern phases can be valuable, particularly when we seek sanctuary and use them as opportunities. During these phases, growth in listening for God's direction and in faith can abound. The key is not to take matters into your own hands. Living through holding pattern phases can be a struggle, and they can be long. After my husband's death, I was placed into a seemingly endless holding pattern known as probate court. We did not have a will and so I entered probate. This is not an area where you should have a time line or be impatient. There is little to do except wait on the legal matters to run their course. I had no control over any of it and could do nothing until it resolved itself. I could not sell any property, change any accounts, or even put my name on the title of my car. I could not do anything. I simply wanted to add caller ID to my home phone account and I couldn't. At a time when I desperately wanted to have some control over something and everything seemed beyond my grasp, I could not even get caller ID. I was thrust into a holding pattern that was indefinite in length. During these past years, I sought sanctuary more often and allowed God to generate growth. I gained the advantage of knowing that it is better to have God in control. I also learned that sitting tight in the holding patterns is an act of faith. Being still is an act of faith that demonstrates a willingness to keep God in control no matter how long the waiting can take. The waiting can be long, but when we become impatient and spring into action, we miss the growth opportunities. We generally produce a mess with our frantic activity.

Why do so many people miss experiencing sanctuary? Choosing sanctuary is hard. In the noise and rush of our lives, habit is to keep moving, generate more sound, and find a faster way. Stopping is hard, quiet is uncomfortable, and so we just press on. Another reason people avoid sanctuary is what I call the Moses response. Hearing direction from God can be scary. Moses demonstrates this. He has sought sanctuary from the noise of Egypt in the desert. One could say that living as a sheepherder was a kind of holding pattern. Then in a moment totally separated from others, on a mountain, he hears a word from God. Moses reacts as we all tend to. "You don't really want me to go for You, do You?" I have had the Moses response to almost every major word of direction I have heard from God. The Moses response is what prevents many of us from going anywhere near a bush that might burn. Take heart, Moses did go where God was sending him–and so can we!

Sanctuary is hard. It is hard for us to choose to be still and listen. It is hard for us to discover what type of sanctuary will allow us to hear God best. It is hard for us to hear a word from God and not react with fear. It is hard to keep sanctuary a top priority. Regardless of all the challenges, it is even more difficult for me to imagine going through these past years without moments of sanctuary daily and journeys of sanctuary annually. There is a difference between those who have been in the presence of God and those who have not. The difference is not in the types of struggles they encounter, but rather in the undeniable peace those who have been in God's presence possess. Shut down the computer, turn off the phones, silence the television, and move into His presence.

Psalm 46:10 "Be still and know that I am God; I will be exalted among the nations, I will be exalted in the earth." (NIV)

The Importance Of Peace

The third Father's Day weekend seemed just as hard as any before. As I went for my Saturday morning run, the loneliness and pain mixed with the concern for my children and the struggle they were experiencing. The mixture became overwhelming, and soon it was difficult to breathe and run because of my crying. All this time has passed, and still I encounter pain that can be as intense as the very first days. Fortunately, another feeling is also as strong now as those first days, peace. There has been and remains a constant peace. I experience God's provision for my every need, and God grants me peace constantly. Not only can God provide and grant peace, God will. I have come this far without lacking divine peace, and it is that peace that gets me through these incredibly hard times.

> *John 14:27 "Peace I leave you: my peace I give you. I do not give to you as the world gives. Do not let your hearts be troubled and do not be afraid." NIV*

The peace I am talking about is not from a relationship with a human; it is not situational being based on job, material possessions, or accomplishments. It is divine peace from God. It transcends human reasoning and comprehension. It is the peace that the apostle Paul speaks about in Scripture. "Grace and peace to you." Paul is also the one who writes in his letter to the Philippians that he has learned to be content in all circumstances. It is a peace that only can come from God. I have discovered the benefits of this peace and have learned that it is ours when we are keeping our hearts, minds, and lives within the will of God. God's peace is what kept me sane when my external world toppled.

Don't confuse this peace with a painless existence or a life of ease. This peace is not about that. Rather the peace brought by the Holy Spirit provides calm and comfort, guidance, and hope. Peace gives us comfort and calm when we are defeated or struggling. During this difficult Father's Day weekend, when loneliness and hurt build up into a tidal wave of despair, peace accomplishes much. Peace helps me stay in the arms of God for comfort. There are other ways a lonely, single woman could seek to solve the ache of loneliness. I don't need to elaborate. Simply watch some evening television, and you will see what I am talking about. Peace keeps me seeking God instead. Peace also generates a calm that prevents frantic, busy activity that is simply a means to avoid pain. I have met many people who struggle with life situations that cause them intense pain. They deal with the pain by running, staying so frantically busy that the hurt cannot touch them. They numb themselves with schedules and fatigue. In the process, they miss the opportunity to confront the pain and allow God to heal them. Worse, they miss the divine peace God is offering during the painful times. The experience of pain, crying, and feeling the peace of God all at once is indescribable and certainly a feeling I have come to treasure. God's peace becomes an anchor, and that generates calm. Yes, the pain and loneliness are just as real, but they are not compounded by frantic nonproductive or even destruction actions.

A deep sense of inner peace from God prevents those leaps into action that many people later regret.

During difficult times of struggle or pain or even frustrating times of lengthy holding patterns in life, peace becomes a crucial component to staying anchored in God. God's peace helps us become at peace with ourselves and our circumstances, making the alone times and waiting times far more tolerable. Peace with ourselves also makes peace with those around us easier.

Peace is as reliable as a compass when we are seeking God's guidance. When we go where God is leading, there is peace, even if we are not excited about where God is leading. As God leads my life to reconstruction and restoration, I have been led by God to make several very difficult decisions. The most difficult of these was to leave my church position as Minister of Music and put the clergy ordination process on hold in the form of a leave of absence. This decision felt like I was being stripped of something that I deeply and dearly loved. There was incredible loss, pain, and hardship in the decision. It felt as though years of seminary work and church service would be thrown aside and become meaningless. My place in my church family would become uncomfortable. My understanding of God's call and claim on my life would become foggy. Amongst all of this struggle and heartache, there was one thing that was unquestionable; I felt God's peace with the decision to resign. I did not have any way to account for the pain or answers for the questions that filled my heart and mind. However, I had an overwhelming sense of peace with the decision. Because of that peace, I did resign and have discovered many blessings that God could not have brought to me if I had remained in that position. I still lack answers regarding the future of my ministerial call, but I do not lack peace.

God's peace is a guiding force. If you are at peace with a

decision or direction, truly wholeheartedly at peace, then there is a very clear directive from God. When I am covered in peace by God, then I know God is in control. I can go where He sends me to serve knowing that I am His and that I am going to be taken care of. This peace defies worldly logic. This peace means I am at peace with resigning a title, a position, and a slot in the timeline of a process toward an accomplishment—all without an end in sight. God's peace assures me that I am His, and it is not what I do or who I am in title or job that matters. It is only Whose I am and from Whom I receive peace and affirmation that matters.

Living in divine peace brings about an abundant joy that makes following God's directions completely worth any cost. God's peace makes hope remain. When our earthly circumstances bring loneliness and tears, fatigue and frustration, sorrow and hurt, peace steps in and sprinkles hope over it all. Regardless of how bleak circumstances may appear to the earthly assessment, hope is there because this is the peace that transcends human understanding. While to the onlooker it may look impossible, the peace that calms and comforts the heart and guides decisions also generates hope. We can hope and have faith. We can be content in all circumstances. We can do this because we are filled with the peace that comes only from God as we keep our hearts and minds on Him and not on the circumstance.

Peace within is what I want. More than any earthly possession, peace is what makes me content. I will follow where God leads so that I can experience His peace. Grace and peace to you.

2 Corinthians 4:8–9 "We are hard pressed on every side, but not crushed; perplexed, but not in despair; persecuted, but not abandoned; struck down, but not destroyed." NIV

The Importance Of Forgiveness

Her words hung in the air and stung. Those painful words came from a dear and trusted friend, and what she said was not meant to hurt, but truth convicts. In her simple statement, "Anger is reasonable, but you can't be insane with anger." She generated a huge turning point for me. Ten months after Elan's death, I thought I was doing a pretty good job of living my life and moving forward in faith. I was not aware that the anger was beginning to cast a shadow over everything I said and did. Anger is the result of not forgiving. When we don't forgive, we get angry. I had not realized how angry I was, and I had not even thought about forgiving.

As my friend and I drove to a weekend spiritual retreat, the conversation turned to how my life was continuing. We talked about work, the kids, and the aspects of living that you would expect two friends to talk about. Somewhere in the conversation, she made this simple statement. God used that statement to open my eyes.

I had not considered forgiveness. In the months after my husband's death, I learned that while he was collecting a water sample at a construction site, the construction company foreman gave instructions to the track hoe driver to bury some large pieces of concrete in a trench. Without checking for my husband's whereabouts, the concrete was buried and so was my husband. I had spent time on grieving, adjusting, and counseling for my children and myself. I had spent time on schedules and maintaining the household. I spent time on health issues. I had not spent time on forgiving.

Now I was confronted with an undeniable reality. Because I had not addressed forgiving, anger was overtaking me. It was affecting my personality, my presence, and my health. I don't recall much of the conversation after her statement. I do recall what God did with it. God began working on my heart. As I started the weekend retreat, I also started a journey with God toward forgiving. As soon as I heard "insane with anger," I was convicted that I needed to listen. Then the conviction focused on forgiveness. I knew where God was leading me, but I did not want to go. The second day of the retreat, after many arguments with God, I prayed earnestly. I asked God to change my heart and my perspective. I asked God to empower me to forgive. I knew that I could not forgive by my own will or strength. God answered my prayer and changed my heart in the most unusual way.

That night as I crawled into my retreat camp bunk, I had a tough time getting comfortable. Not because it wasn't my own bed, but because I had forgotten my razor. The hair on my legs was irritating and my thoughts turned to shaving my legs. I longed for a razor and some relief. It is amazing what God can use. As I focused on my shaving need, the men responsible for my husband's death came to mind. I'm certain God led my thoughts as they moved from shaving, to those men, to their daily shaving, to their daily requirement to face themselves in the mirror knowing they are responsible for a good man's death. I don't know how long I lay there in the dark on the top bunk in that cabin, but during that time, God changed my heart. I thought about the daily routine of shaving each man goes through. I thought of these men, looking at themselves daily and knowing what they were seeing. Compassion began growing in my heart. God changed my heart and replaced the anger with compassion.

The next day I began forgiveness. Because of the amazing power of God, I have forgiven the track hoe driver, the supervisor, and the owner of the construction company responsible for my husband's death. That weekend was a turning point for me. Moreover, it only happened by the power of God to change my heart. God convicted me of my need to forgive and then empowered me to do so. That is the awesome power of God. God empowered me to do that which seemed absolutely impossible. Forgiveness was a part of God's plan to restore my life and the lives of my children. My forgiveness did nothing for the men I forgave, but forgiving was a blessing God gave me.

James 1:20 "For man's anger does not bring about the righteous life that God desires." NIV

Hatred, bitterness, and anger are overwhelmingly heavy loads to carry around with you daily. God wants better for us. That is one reason we are instructed to forgive. The load of anger and bitterness can generate emotional problems as well as health and other physical problems. It is simply not healthy mentally, physically, or spiritually to carry hatred, bitterness, and anger. God does more than simply telling us to forgive. God is ready to make forgiveness happen by changing our hearts, our perspectives, and our thoughts. Forgiveness is a blessing to the one actively forgiving. It changed me for the better. God's help came when I willingly opened myself to His help in forgiving. I had to have a willingness to approach forgiveness, and then God could have that part of my heart and change it. This did not only occur with those responsible for my husband's death; it has occurred in smaller matters as well. As the majority of my friends fell away in the wake of my tragedy, God enabled forgiveness there also. God changed my heart and perspective, allowing me to see the pain and difficulty those past friends suffered in watching my struggle. God filled my heart with compassion for those friends, and replaced the loneliness with understanding. In doing that, God shaped my heart for new friendships. Opening my heart for God to enable forgiveness became much more of a blessing for me than the forgiveness could ever have mattered to those I forgave.

Jesus tells us to forgive seventy times seven, not because that generates a magic forgiveness quotient. No, the point is this: Instead of counting and tracking out the forgiveness, we should adopt an attitude of willingness to forgive. Do not calculate and formulate mercy, but rather, have a willing heart to be truly merciful, then God can empower the rest.

God knew that forgiving would free us and empower the Holy Spirit in our lives. We need not confuse forgiveness with reconciliation or approval. God does not call us to blindly approve of the actions of those who hurt us or generate tragedy. Nor does God direct us to build relationships with those who wrong us. Forgiveness does not imply or require approval. Forgiveness, instead, is a product of our willingness to allow God to change our hearts and replace our anger with compassion. We are then able to have healthier relationships with others and, most importantly, with God.

Forgiveness goes still further. Forgiveness demonstrates a reverence for God and God's divine authority as the judge. We attempt a certain level of judgeship when we determine that the anger and condemnation we feel is ours to hold and maintain.

The men responsible for my husband's death had to come to peace with God regarding what they did. They did not have to come to peace with me. God's work on my heart to enable me to forgive them became an act of reverence for God's authority in this area. As I forgave, I affirmed that the peace was to be made between those men and God and not with me. Forgiving those men doesn't say that I think they were right. Forgiving them says that I know that God will do what is right in the aftermath. I have experienced just that—God has done what is right for me, my children, and in the lives of many others involved. God has done not only what is right, but more importantly, God has done what is best.

God will do what is best for you and what is right. More than that, you will never be asked to forgive more than what was already forgiven on Calvary. Forgiving allowed me to be open to God's guidance and leading during the trial. After forgiving, I realized that the wrongful death trial was the only means to allow those responsible for Elan's death to do what our society allows in making retribution. Without a wrongful death case, those men would have to live with their wrongdoing without any opportunity to relieve the guilt. God used the trial as a time to permit them to remove the guilt from a permanent place in their lives. Now they can face themselves in the mirror each morning to shave and not question what they see.

Additionally, forgiving freed me of any need for "getting even." The trial could be placed in God's hands. I did not need anything from it. I came to understand that the trial process was about God making peace with the hearts of the responsible men. I was free to listen to God and hear from Him when the trial process was complete. It was God's work, not my need to play out anger or vengeance. In the end, divine peace was the reward.

Forgiving became a turning point for me. God was working to restore my life, but I could not make a critical choice until I forgave. Forgiving is the predecessor to choosing happiness. You're not free to make the choice of living, laughing, and happiness until you choose to allow God to empower you to forgive. Once you have given God his authority as judge, allowed Him to change your heart, and you have forgiven, then the choices begin. You can set aside anger and pick up joy. You can learn to see that what you have in blessings and faith is more important than what you don't have. This is a huge move. To come to the place where you realize that your relationship with God and the faith you have is truly the most important thing. You cannot look with thankfulness and joy at what you have until you first forgive regarding what you don't have or have lost.

Forgiveness is not a one-time act. It is a process. Anger still creeps in. I see my son do something amazing, I watch my daughter receive an award, and suddenly the absence of their dad brings sharp pain, and I have to stop, pray, and forgive again.

I don't know how many times I will forgive again, but I'm sure that those men are still shaving each day. I am completely resolved on two things: The peace they must make is with God, not me, and I will choose to forgive by the power of God and choose happiness.

Matthew 11:28 "Come to me all you that are weary and are carrying heavy burdens, and I will give you rest." NRSV

God Speaks In Acts Of Compassion

Sitting out at the job site where Elan's body was eventually found became the only thing I could do in the days between his death and the police uncovering his body. During those days, a cold front came through. Each day was more bitterly cold and more miserable than the day before. A group of friends would sit with me each day. One day they arrived with thermoses full of coffee and hot chocolate from the coffee shop in the grocery store near my house. It was a gift from the shop manager and a sign of God's hand. A pastor from a nearby church arrived with hand warmers, gloves, and lunches. Again, God revealed His presence in this act of compassion and spoke to my heart, reminding me that I was not alone. There were thousands more of these words from God. Meals were brought from neighbors and members of a church in the community. My church home housed and fed family members in from out of town. Dry goods, paper goods, and even dog snacks for my pets were brought to the house. I experienced help in a myriad of ways. Each is an example of the many acts of compassion given. Shortly after the funeral, a friend came to my home with donuts on a Saturday morning to baby-sit so I could get out and do my yard work, which I loved doing. Over and over, God spoke to me with acts of compassion. Students from my school organized cards, notes, and gifts to demonstrate love and support. Money was raised to assist my family. Constantly God spoke and through these acts; I clearly heard Him say that He was still my God and would sustain my family and me. The acts of compassion continued as a dear friend played God's love on the piano at Elan's funeral and a large choir of high school students sang, simply because I asked.

In the months and years since the funeral, more compassionate acts spoke God's words to me and my children in people who helped me keep my house maintained, people who hung my Christmas lights, and through the husband of a soccer playing teammate who would come to the games to watch my children so I could play. Many of these still continue today, and God continues to remind me that He is my provider and sustainer. Phone calls and visits spoke God's love. I was constantly surrounded by God's voice, and I still hear His voice, in the acts of care and compassion of those God sends to minister to us. God adamantly wants me to know that He will not forsake me. I am not alone.

God generates compassion. It is a gift of the Holy Spirit. It is also a motivator. God-powered compassion moves people into action and speaks to the hurting heart in a way that words fail to accomplish. When God motivated a church member to spend the night in his truck in my driveway so I would feel safe, I heard God say, "I will not forsake you." No words could have spoken what those actions did. When a community church provided food for two and a half months, I lived God's promise of care and provision beyond what words can tell.

Compassion is the motivator that activates God's provision. God steps in through these acts of compassion and demonstrates in a tangible way His ability to sustain us. The understanding that God can sustain was no longer a theological premise or a strong belief, rather it was an active reality.

In tragedy, we often hear of those who question God's role. Where was God? I contend that when we look into the eyes of those who act out of compassion during our darkest times, we see the eyes of God. Those people show us where God is. I know that I have looked into the eyes of God more times than I can innumerate, and I continue to experience God daily via compassionate acts. Not only have I looked into God's eyes, I have heard his voice. I hear God telling me that I will be provided for, not left alone, and that to Him, I am valuable and lovely. This is a huge message in the loneliness and overwhelming circumstances of raising two children as a widow. God continues to speak to me and remind me of these things in the acts of those in my life. A phone call, a card in the mail that says I'm thought of; all these are divinely motivated acts of compassion that speak to my heart and assure me of God's love.

During the days the police searched for Elan, I felt as though God was silent. I did not want to hear God's initial words of the earliest moments, when my heart knew I had been widowed. Instead, I chose to hear what I wanted to. I decided to look for a missing person. Even though I chose not to hear God's message, God continued to speak in acts of compassion, and I accused God of being silent. There is no possible way for me to recall the thousands of acts of compassion that were showered on me and my family during those days that I was certain I could not hear God. God was not silent. God was showering me with the message that no matter how horrific this tragedy seemed, He could lift me out of it, carry me through it, and provide for all of my needs and the needs of my family. God spoke volumes during those days. I, however, was waiting for the huge miracle message, the booming voice, the lightning strike, or at least a clear message in a dream.

I don't think I am that different from others who have endured tragedy. We look for the big voice answer; all the while, God is sending volumes of information in the acts of compassion of His servants around us. It is not that God was silent; it was that I was not listening. All around me, through thousands of acts of compassion, God spoke.

As God has carried me through this time and moved me forward, those compassionate acts and the messages they carried have taught me and equipped me to act when motivated by God to extend His compassion to others. Having been in a position where acts of compassion were the messages of God, I no longer ignore the impulse to extend such acts. Instead of moving past an opportunity to act, I listen. At some junctions, I do not feel moved to action, and then I know that my hands are not needed there. In other situations, I feel motivated to act. In years past, I might have felt motivated and sometimes responded. Other times I did not respond. Now having experienced the impact of acts of compassion, I don't hesitate when I feel motivated to step in. Usually I find that when I am motivated and I act, I am uniquely equipped to provide what is needed for the situation. Sometimes we are motivated to just listen, run an errand, or share a meal. These simple acts can be our calling to represent a message from God. Other times the call to action can be more significant. When driving my daughter to her diving lesson, we came upon an auto accident that had just happened. I was compelled to stop, despite not knowing how I could help with two children in my car and no emergency training. In the end, it became apparent to me that the young mother involved in the accident needed some-one just like me. Her two children played with my two children while the accident was cleared. I had the honor of praying with her and her children before I drove her home. I really did not feel like I would be able to help in any way, but I felt led to stop. I stopped. Years ago I would have placed the schedule of diving lessons and the demands of my day in front of being led to stop and help. I would have reasoned that there was nothing I could do to help. I would have gone past and missed the opportunity to be a tool for God. Now I know how much people need to hear from God, and I know how clearly God can speak to us through the simplest acts of compassion. Reasons like schedule or feeling like what we have to offer is inadequate should not stop us from acting on the motivations we receive.

When we do act, we benefit as well, in many ways. It is hard to help others when we are carrying burdens God would have us put down. When we are preoccupied with our own troubles, we are not free to help others. God calls us to acts of compassion to encourage us to hand off our troubles to Him to carry. We can't continue to carry our own burdens and move in the directions God would send us for healing and restoration for ourselves. When we act out of divinely inspired compassion, we are motivated to put down our burdens, and we are blessed with a sense of purpose for God. More is given to us than we give. Important in this is that we gain the opportunity to pass off our burdens and hurts to God. When we do this, when we give our hurts and weaknesses to God, He can be glorified in His strength to care for us and heal us as well as in His demonstrations of care for others through us.

There is a lot written and said about nonverbal communication between people. As disciples, we must not overlook our call to participate in God's nonverbal communication to his children. That nonverbal communication is the divinely inspired acts of compassion we experience and are called to be a part of. Listen to God by looking around.

Following God's Voice Into Ministry

When I was growing up, the pastor of my church seemed so strong and so wise. He was, and still is. What I didn't realize then, but have come to learn since, is that his strength and wisdom came out of his life experiences and struggles. This is true for all of us. Strength, perspective, wisdom, and a myriad of other virtues do not come from a book or a seminary, nor are they inborn. We are all like coal needing the pressure and heat to, through time, transform us into the diamond God had in mind when He created us.

We are all ministers in some capacity or another. This happens when we choose discipleship. Few carry the title of ordained minister, but all who believe have a ministry. Our life experiences and deepest wounds become our strengths for ministry. Your ministry, and mine, is most effective when it comes out of those wounds. Jesus demonstrated this best. All of His teachings, parables, and miracles were, and are, significant. Nevertheless, Jesus' wounds on the cross at Calvary were His ministry and our salvation. Our life experiences bump and bruise us. Our life tragedies shatter us. That is when it is most vital that we step up in faith, follow where God leads, allow God to be the master healer, and allow God to lead us into the ministry He can create for us.

Scripture contains a wonderful, but brief story that captures this idea. There is a huge crowd; Jesus is on his way to an important place. She is not important. In fact, she is an outcast and should not even be in the crowd. She had been bleeding for years and had tried every possible cure. Because of her bleeding, she was unclean. This separated her from the "clean" members of society. She longed for her misery to end. She longed to be healed. She took a huge risk. She stepped out in faith. She knew that if she were caught in the crowd, if the risk did not pay off, she would be much worse off than before. Yet she acted on her faith. She pushed through the crowd. Jesus stopped and asked who had touched his robe. Jesus responded by meeting her need and healing her, but he did not stop there. Jesus commended her for her faith and for acting on it.

Scripture doesn't tell us what happens to the woman years later. I imagine that she was able to minister to the hurting and outcast in a different way than those who had never hurt or been outcast. I also imagine that she told many people about the results of acting on faith. I also surmise that despite all of the hurt and pain of her past, because she reached out in faith, God made her whole and set her into action.

I have experienced the effectiveness of ministry through wounds. A couple of years before my husband's death, an ex-student of mine lost her Dad. I was notified and went to visit her and her mom. I kept in touch with them. When my husband was killed, she and her Mom became a hugely effective ministry team for me. She would share with me anything my children might need, and her Mom seemed to know my needs even before I did. Her mom sent me books, cards, and gifts. She had me out to their home for a weekend to just get away and talk. She understood my needs and could meet them. Those two ladies, as hurt as they had been, were the most effective ministers I encountered. The amazing part is that God was not done there. About a year after my husband's death, a friend and coworker lost her husband. By example of the ministry I had experienced and the lessons of my own hurt, I knew what to do. God put on my heart the desire to minister to my work associate. God heals, repairs, and then calls us into action.

At some point in all our lives, we are like the woman in the crowd—feeling broken, outcast, and as if there is no solution. I have been there. My heart and life looked like a shattered window on the floor, and no one had a solution but God. Piece by piece, God has picked up those shards of glass and is putting them back together like a master craftsman. The picture has changed, and I don't exactly know what this new picture will be, but I know Whom to trust. Just like the woman, our only solution is to push through the crowds of depression, chaos, confusion, and despair and reach out in faith to the Master Healer.

That is hard to do. We want to be the one generating our solution. Yet we are shattered and would be better off to confess that we do not know our own answers and cannot put the pieces together ourselves. To reach out to God, trust enough to act on faith alone, and risk a great deal is hard! The woman in the crowd shows us that the hard act of following in faith can be done. As we follow, led by prayer, the Holy Spirit, and the God-inspired directions spoken by others, we see that this Scripture is one we can live. Christ will respond to our needs and commend our acting on faith. We can, by the power of Christ, be made whole. The Master Craftsman needs us to follow in faith, and He will put together a stained glass window that will cause others to say, "Just look at what God has done!"

Following in faith is hard, and at times, it can cause us to step into frightening crowds. In the time I have been allowing God to put the pieces of my life back together to form His will of a portrait, I have been called to follow into some scary places. I have followed into some public speaking engagements that were a whole new "scary crowd" for me. I was led to leave a job I loved, a church congregation I loved, and even to build a new house. I have been led to release many dear and special friendships as well. Each time I follow and respond in faith, I experience healing and can see new images appearing in the window under construction. Time required performing the job I left has been put to use in counseling sessions and precious time spent with my children. New worship experiences have allowed God to touch my heart in new and different ways. New friendships have entered my life and have grown and strengthened. Each time I am asked to push through the crowd and act on faith and I do, I see the picture in the new stained glass window take on more shape.

The picture of my life will never again be the same as it was before. I do not know what it will become. With God in charge of the reconstruction, I do know that it can shine and glorify Him. I can trust God to construct the window because I know that at Calvary, God's heart hurt far worse than mine ever has. I can give Him my pain and know that He will care for me, heal me, and make me whole. Our task is to reach out with faith. Once healed, go forth declaring the amazing power of God to accomplish all of this. Once we have touched the robe of Christ, we cannot stop there. The task is then to go forward and answer God's call to minister wherever we are sent. Most importantly, if that ministry is born out of the wounds we have endured, embrace it.

Psalm 19:1 "The heavens declare the glory of God; the skies proclaim the work of his hands." NIV

Choose Happiness

I'm sitting in the office of a friend I don't see often, catching up on life's events since we last met. Many years of hard work and dedication have gone into his very successful business career, yet he will be retired soon. He is far too young to be retired. While many hope to be able to retire early and enjoy life, they also want to be in control of the decision. He and I both know the same truth. At some point in everyone's life, a situation you did not want or choose will be perpetrated upon you, and you will have no control over choosing that circumstance. Difficult and tragic situations come into our lives. Most of the time, we have no hand in setting them into motion. All of them, we have no control over. We only have control over one choice. We can choose God and the sacred joy and happiness that come with that relationship. The moment of control comes when you choose to give control to God and choose sacred happiness within the peace that transcends understanding.

We cannot always choose our circumstance, but we can choose our response. We cannot always choose what this world hands us, but we can choose what we hand to those we love and those around us. As I sat in my home planning my husband's funeral, I remember thinking that this was not the way it was supposed to be. I had married a good man who dedicated himself to being my partner in a wonderful marriage. I will never have a 50th wedding anniversary now, and I was supposed to. My children will not know the amazing, godly man their father was, and they were supposed to. At that moment, there came the pivotal choice. I even spoke it aloud to my mom. I decided that although I had many reasons to live in sorrow and self-pity, I chose happiness. I decided that I would be intentional about choosing happiness.

The error many self-help practitioners make is just that, the self-help approach. Yes, I choose happiness, but I cannot make myself happy. Only God can give me the provisions, guidance, and peace to be truly happy.

I still have reasons for sorrow and self-pity. Some are big, like loneliness and no husband to talk to when making significant decisions regarding my children. Some are more moderate, such as suffering a panic attack when I left my children with my parents so I could travel with the high school choir. Others are small, like the time I had to handle the iced-over driveway myself. However, each of these, regardless of the magnitude, must be met the same way, with prayer, by handing them to God, and with a commitment to choose happiness.

Psalm 30:11 "You have turned my mourning into dancing; You have taken off my sackcloth and have clothed me with joy." NRSV

When we turn to God to bring us into happiness, we hand Him our heart and allow Him to begin a process of reconstruction. God changes our hearts and brings us into divine joy that bypasses earthly reason. This decision to allow God to change me, to reconstruct my heart, is repeated almost daily. As new challenges arise, producing new reasons that I could turn to sorrow or self-pity, I must recommit myself to allowing God's reconstruction to continue. The more I allow God to change me, the more divine joy I can experience.

In Luke 24:13–32, we see the story of the disciples on the road to Emmaus after the Crucifixion and Resurrection. Jesus walks with them and talks with them. These men are so engrossed in the devastating events of the past days that they do not recognize Jesus is walking there with them. They see just another traveler. They are blinded because of where their minds are focused. No matter what events we have been through, as we walk, Jesus is with us. We must make the choice not to be blind to that.

Choosing happiness, trusting God for divine joy is a tremendous act of faith. We must move in that direction no matter how insurmountable the sorrow seems. Between Venice, Italy, and Vienna, Austria, stand the Alps. In an effort to connect the two cities, a rail project was begun. The problem? No train was powerful enough to pull through the mountains. Tracks were laid anyway, knowing that someday there would be a train that could make the trip. Sometimes our sorrow is as impassable as those mountains. Faith lays the tracks.

We all know people who have made the other choice–the one of sorrow and self-pity. They may wear that choice as a garment of bitterness and anger or as a badge of the one who is a victim. Perhaps it's a veil of "if only" that you see when you meet them. All of us know someone who has chosen sorrow and is now an empty-shell person. Empty-shell people have many different outward appearances. Some are obvious; some are camouflaged by busyness or humor. The shell, whether obvious or camouflaged, covers emptiness for all of them. You wonder what happened. The answer is consistently the same. We all come to a crossroad—to turn and choose emptiness, sorrow, and self-pity or to choose to trust God for divine joy and happiness. I know the day I stood at that crossroad and I chose happiness. Some know when they chose, others do not. One thing to keep in mind is that the choice for happiness can always be made. If you haven't chosen it yet, it is not too late.

The pivotal issue, at the center of the choice, is trusting God to do for you and with you that which is good. We need to pray for his good. Don't confuse what is good. Good is not an easy way out of trials. Good is not prosperity or God's indulgence. God's good is transformation. We should pray for God to transform us, not indulge us. Pray for strength and transformation through the trials, and pray to have an impact for the Kingdom of God. This is too important to gloss over—*pray to be an impact on the Kingdom of God.*

Many people feel that happiness will come when they can enjoy financial prosperity, but if you allow God to transform you for divine joy, you will seek impact prosperity instead. Regardless of your profession, you are called and created to be a part of God's purpose here on earth. This is the opportunity to participate in something eternal, not earthly. We are each designed for God's ideal will for our lives. That is the place where you are not only living in relationship with God, but you are living the abundant joy of submitting your life to living God's ideal will for you. That is where you make an impact. That is where you enjoy impact prosperity. This is a different way of assessing prosperity. This generates a God centered way of experiencing joy. We mustn't pray for indulgence, but rather transformation to become what God had in mind when He created us. God's transformation and our living in His ideal will for our lives involves endurance for the hard times—not an easy ride, impact for an eternal Kingdom—not earthly fame, and abundant joy—not necessarily abundant cash flow.

When we choose happiness, choosing to put our hearts in God's hands for reconstruction, we choose to submit our lives to the ideal will of God. In living out God's ideal will for our lives, we experience impact prosperity and divine, sacred joy.

When people look at my life and my circumstances, I do not want them to feel sorry for me or to pity me. Although each time I tell someone I am a widow the response is, "I'm sorry." I do not want people to see me and feel pity. Rather, I want people to see me and see the miracle God has done in the lives of my children and in my life. I want them to see a living message in us that proclaims—God is good all the time! I want them to see happiness brought forth by God. I want them to see how good God is and what God can do. I want them to marvel at God! God has lifted me out of the muddiest, darkest, most pitiful, and sorrowful place I could have imagined. More than that, God has put a song in my heart. For each one of us, divine, sacred joy is one choice away.

Isaiah 55:12 "For you shall go out in joy, and be led back in peace." NRSV

Contact Julie Ann Allen
or order more copies of this book at

TATE PUBLISHING, LLC

127 East Trade Center Terrace
Mustang, Oklahoma 73064

(888) 361 - 9473

Tate Publishing, LLC

www.tatepublishing.com